Remarks On the Construction of Hothouses

REMARKS
ON
HOTHOUSES,
&c.

JP

REMARKS
ON
HOTHOUSES,
&c.

REMARKS
ON
THE CONSTRUCTION
OF
HOTHOUSES,

POINTING OUT

THE MOST ADVANTAGEOUS FORMS, MATERIALS, AND
CONTRIVANCES TO BE USED IN THEIR CONSTRUCTION;

ALSO

A REVIEW

OF THE VARIOUS METHODS OF BUILDING THEM IN FOREIGN
COUNTRIES AS WELL AS IN ENGLAND:

With Ten Plates, from Etchings on Stone.

By J. C. LOUDON, F.L.S.

MEMBER OF THE IMPERIAL SOCIETY, MOSCOW; OF THE NATURAL HISTORY SOCIETY, BERLIN;
AND OF THE POTSDAM ROYAL ŒCONOMICAL SOCIETY, ETC. ETC.

"The Public have still much to learn on the subject of Hothouses."
  Sir Joseph Banks on the *Forcing Houses of the Romans*.

London:

PRINTED FOR J. TAYLOR, AT THE ARCHITECTURAL LIBRARY,
No. 59, HIGH HOLBORN,

BY RICHARD AND ARTHUR TAYLOR, SHOE-LANE.

1817.

Rd
L92 R

TO

THE RIGHT HONOURABLE

SIR JOSEPH BANKS, BART. K.G.C.B.

ONE OF HIS MAJESTY'S MOST HONOURABLE PRIVY COUNCIL,

PRESIDENT OF THE ROYAL SOCIETY, TRUST. BRIT. MUS. ETC. ETC.

S*IR*,

I have been induced to dedicate this Work to you, because the subject on which it treats has been illustrated by you in one of the few instances in which you have favoured the world with the productions of your pen.

Some of the plans which I recommend are new; and as I am desirous of introducing them only so far as they will stand the test of impartial and enlightened examination, to whom could I have dedicated this Work with so much propriety as to one who possesses the wisdom of age without its prejudices, and retains the candour of youth without its rashness?

I have the honour to be,

S*IR*,

Your most obliged

and most obedient humble Servant,

J. C. LOUDON.

B*AYSWATER* H*OUSE*,
25th April 1817.

CONTENTS.

PART I.

ON THE PRINCIPLES OF CONSTRUCTION.

	Page.
Origin of the Horticultural Societies	1
Early attention of these societies to artificial climates	2
Attention of scientific men and gardeners, previously to the establishment of these societies, to the subject of hothouses	2
Mr. Knight's improvements and writings the most important in respect to hothouses	3
Important principle of the slope of the roof introduced by Mr. Knight	3
Boerhaave the first who laid down principles for the slope of glass	4
Linnæus	5
Adanson	5
Nicholas Facio de Douillier	6
Laurence, Bradley, London and Wise, Switzer, Miller	7
Mr. Knight applied the principle to forcing houses, and illustrated it more fully	8
Mr. Wilkinson's formula for the application of the principle	10
Sir George Mackenzie's extension of the principle	13
Examination of the form of house proposed by Sir George Mackenzie	17
Suggestions for the improvement of this plan	21
Curved roofs applied to longitudinal hothouses	23
Description of vineries and peach-houses on this construction	23
Description of the arrangement suitable for a pinery on this plan	29
Arrangement for opening the sashes in houses of this description	32
Great advantage of metallic sashes over wooden ones	34
Comparative advantages of different descriptions of glass roofs	35
Outer or inner curtain recommended for hothouses	38
Objections to the use of metals in the roofing of hothouses answered	41

PART II.

ON THE DETAIL OF CONSTRUCTION, AND ON EXECUTION.

	Page
INTRODUCTORY REMARKS	47
Of the SITUATION chosen for hothouses	49
Count Razumowski's hothouses at Gorinka near Moscow	49
Of the DESIGN	50
Leading data on the subject of design	51
Of HEATING HOTHOUSES	52
By fire	52
By steam	53
By dung and by other modes	53
Of HEATING BY STEAM	54
Comparison between steam and fire heat	55
Objections to the use of steam	57
Heating by fire heat for common purposes	59
Of VENTILATION	65
Dr. Anderson's mode	66
Mr. Stuart's	66
Mr. Stratt's of Derby	66
Marquis de Chabannes'	67
Mr. Benford Deacon's	68
A mode for ordinary purposes	69
Of ARTIFICIAL REGULATION	71
Mr. Kewley's apparatus	71
Of EXECUTION	72
Masonry	72
Woodwork	73
Metallic work	74
Metallic sashes	76
Metallic bars or astragals	78
Wooden sashes	82
Glazing	83
HOTBEDS	86
HOTWALLS	88

The Plates are printed by Mr. Daniel Redman of Somers Town, from sketches made on stone by the author, and are calculated for illustration rather than embellishment.

REMARKS.

PART I.

On the Principles of CONSTRUCTION, &c.

PERHAPS at no period since the days of Evelyn and Miller has horticulture assumed so respectable an attitude among rural and œconomical pursuits as at the present time. The horticultural societies of London and Edinburgh, composed of men of rank and influence, scientific amateurs, and practical gardeners, give a degree of eclat and salutary consequence to the study; and from this circumstance, as well as the known skill and activity of many of their members, the public may expect to reap considerable advantage.

The origin of these associations, as well as of the present taste for horticulture, may in a great degree be ascribed to the physiological inquiries of Mr. Knight, the president of the London Society; and to the taste and patronage of Sir Joseph Banks. To Mr. Knight the philosopher is indebted for some interesting experiments on the vegetable œconomy communicated from time to time during the last twenty years to the Royal Society; and the gardener for much scientific discussion and valuable practical instruction relative to the culture of fruits, contained in his " Treatise on the Apple and Pear," and in various papers in the London Horticultural Transactions;—the result of this gentleman's enthusiastic pursuit of a favourite study for many years. The taste, judgement, and influence, of Sir Joseph Banks, especially in whatever relates to the study of Nature; his unequalled library in that branch of science; and his friendly protection of those who devote themselves to its study; are too well known to require eulogium. It is justly remarked by an accomplished agricultural writer, that by the devotion of a long life and ample fortune to the pursuit and encouragement of a useful and peaceful branch of human knowledge, he has obtained honour, enjoyed self-satisfaction, and laid the foundation of a fame as extended as civilization, and as permanent as the history of letters[1].

It may readily be supposed that the subject of artificial climates, which by enabling the horticulturist to exhibit spring and summer in the midst of winter, and bring to perfection the delicious fruits and splendid flowers of the torrid zone in a temperate or cold country,—which gives man so proud a command over Nature, and renders a skilful practitioner in such requisition among the opulent,—would receive an early attention from these societies. Accordingly we find Mr. Knight, in his introduction to the published Transactions of the London Society, doubting as to the perfection of the construction of hothouses, "two of which," he observes, "are rarely constructed alike, though intended for the same purpose:" and among the papers subsequently given to the world, are some valuable communications on the subject by the same philosopher, and by Sir Joseph Banks, Mr. Wilkinson, Mr. Williams, Sir George Mackenzie, and several others.

The increasing taste for exotic botany, and more general demand for the culinary luxuries of hothouses, had, previously to the establishment of the London Horticultural Society, produced considerable emulation among scientific men and gardeners, relative to the improvement of their construction. Besides various local alterations, attended with different degrees of success, patents were taken out by Mr. Hoyle,

---

[1] Dr. Anderson in *Recreations in Agriculture and Natural History*.

Dr. Anderson, Mr. Stuart, Mr. Jorden, and subsequently by Mr. Weeks, Mr. Kewley, and others. Some of these inventions have not had sufficient trial, and others have by ulterior changes been long since "*réduits au mérite historique.*"

Of these improvements, and of the various papers published by the horticultural societies, none are more calculated to promote the art of perfecting artificial climates, than the communications of Mr. Knight " on the construction of peach-houses and vineries[1];" and the discussion to which these papers have given rise, on the slope which the glass roofs of hothouses ought to have, in order to receive the greatest possible benefit from the sun's rays at the proper season of the year.

The important principle of adapting the slope of the glass to the object in view, thus recognised and established by Mr. Knight, has long been known to scientific men on the continent, and more or less generally in Britain since Miller's time. It must be confessed, however, that in this country and for the last half century it has been almost wholly lost sight of, or neglected as of little importance. In this period, that description of glass houses, adapted for forcing or maturing tender fruits, had greatly increased. It became the fashion to have hothouses; and these edifices, from being the study of the philosopher, became articles of trade, and taste and science gave way to number and magnitude.

Horticulture improved by the Flemings was in great repute in all the Low Countries during the seventeenth century[2]. Botanic gardens, which were first established in Italy about the middle of the sixteenth century[3], soon found their way there. That of Leyden was founded in 1575, and the celebrated L'Ecluse caused to be constructed in it a conservatory in 1599. A century afterwards (about 1709) six houses of different descriptions for the protection of exotics were erected un-

---

[1] London *Hort. Trans.* vol. i.
[2] Lobel, *Histoire des Plantes*, 1576.
[3] Zannoni, *Istoria Botanica*, Bologna, 1675.

der the direction of the younger Clusius and of the celebrated Boerhaave[1].

BOERHAAVE in designing these houses seems to have been the first to establish a principle for determining the slope of glass, which he develops in his System of Chemistry[2], and which are designated in the *Amœnitates Academicæ*[3], and in the *Encyclopédie Méthodique*[4], "the laws of Boerhaave." Illustrating the laws of light in its passage through glass, he observes, that gardeners often feel the bad effects of placing the upright sashes of conservatories in such a position as that the sun's rays do not pass through them perpendicularly, and consequently that much of the upper part of the house is deprived of his influence. He recommends erecting the glass windows to an angle of 14 deg. 30 min. in those countries where the elevation of the pole is 52¼ deg. for reasons easily deduced from astronomy and dialling[5].

---

[1] See *Index Plantarum*, &c. and also the preface to *Index alter Plantarum quæ in Horto Academico Lugduno-Batavo aluntur conser. ab H. Boerhaave* 1720. The following are the houses alluded to:
Hortus adonidis cum supposito caldario primus.
Hortus adonidis alter magno tepidario hypogeo instructus.
Horti adonidis minores fenestris vitreis et ligneis defensi.
Hortus adonidis maximus fornace calescens.
Pergula hybernaculum præbens variis fornacibus instructum.
Hybernaculum priore calidius.
In the two first of these houses the fire was lighted in a vault; the third had no fire, and the three last were heated by upright German stoves without horizontal flues. This celebrated garden is still visited by the curious. In 1814 it was rather in a state of decay, probably from want of funds, though under the direction of an intelligent old Scotch gardener. It may be necessary to remark, for those who are unaccustomed to botanical latin, that *Garden of Adonis* is a generic term for every description of glass case for preserving or cultivating plants. See a technical arrangement of horticulture in *Amœnitates Academicæ*, tom. iv. p. 211.

[2] *Elementa Chemiæ*, Lugd. Bat. 1732, tom. i. p. 213.

[3] Tom. i. *Descriptio Horti Upsaliensis.*

[4] *Volume d'Aratoire et du Jardinage*, art. "Serre."

[5] "*Oportet hæc hybernacula, directe meridiei opposita, instruere fenestris e vitro erectis ad angulum 14 gr. 30' usque ad pavimentum, iisque pellucidis, si fieri potest. Postea autem lacunar debet ita fieri, ut a linea horizontali, ducta ab altitudine luminum, a fenestris parietem*

(5)

We find LINNÆUS in 1745 approving of the garden of Leyden in the arrangement of that at Upsal[1], and stating in his description of the Caldarium, or dry stove, which he erected there in 1740, the advantages of the particular slope which he had fixed on for the glass roof[2]; no doubt from consulting the laws of Boerhaave, of whose slope for an orangery in latitude 52¼ he gives a diagram in a plate.

ADANSON is the next Continental author of importance who has touched on this subject. In his "*Familles des Plantes*" published in 1763, he has given the first systematic treatise on the theory and practice of constructing hothouses, that probably ever was published. Botanic stoves and greenhouses were the description he had chiefly in view, and these he says ought to be so contrived as to have most sun when the plants are in them. He recommends the use of front glass only; placed upright, or at such an angle as that the sun should be perpendicular to it in November, December, January, and February. The perpendicularity of the glass, he says, protects from the cold occasioned by falling dews. He recommends iron astragals and Bohemian glass in order to obtain the most light possible. "Sloping sashes," he adds, "whether convex or a part of a circle, and of which they cover each part with straw mats as the sun leaves it, or simply inclined so as the rays of the sun may be perpendicular to them in the beginning of March, are only good for that month and for April.

"In general," he concludes, "it will be more advantageous to in-

---

posteriorem versus, deorsum declinet angulo pariter 20 gr. 30' in regionibus ubi elevatio poli est 52¼. *Ratio ex astronomicis et gnomonicis, facilis eruenda hic brevitatis gratia omittitur."*
—*Elementa Chemiæ*, Lugd. Bat. 1732.

[1] *Amœnitates*, tom. i. p. 44.

[2] "*Latus australe Caldarii sola fenestrarum junctura constat hunc in modum inclinatis quem declarat delineatio, in fine hujus opusculi sita, quemque hoc majore adnotatione dignum existimavi, quod Caldarium hac inclinatione fenestrarum, sole radios evibrante, duntaxat ab illo, tantum caloris adquirit, gradum ut thermometrum ad gradus* 30 (that of Celsius is here used) *sæpe adscendat, quamvis non facile* 20 *a* 25 *admittitur superare gradum hortulani vigilantia; nec infra* 15 *gr. hyeme facile descendere, antequam focus defectum solis suppleat.*"—Tom. I. p. 39.

cline the floor of hothouses to the sun's rays in February, which is the time when the plants of the torrid zone, shut up during five months, suffer the most, than to incline the glass frames."

Notwithstanding his own opinion, however, he gives rules, tables, and diagrams, for constructing hothouses to suit every possible situation, from the pole to the equator. In some of these the sloping glass forms the hypothenuse of a triangle; in others part of a trapezium, a segment of a circle, or part of a polygon[1]. The ground plan also varies from a segment of a circle to a parallelogram.

NICHOLAS FACIO DE DOUILLIER[2] is the first writer who appears to have treated the subject of the solar influence in ripening fruits in this country. This author, who was tutor to the Marquis of Tavistock, and a fellow of the Royal Society, published his treatise in 1699: he does not however enter on the subject of hothouses directly, though the greater part of what he states respecting the comparative advantages of perpendicular and sloping walls will equally apply to sloping or perpendicular glass roofs. It appears that this work was, at the time it was published rejected by practical men, but it is replete with ingenuity and mathematical demonstration; and, with the faci-

---

[1] "*Les meilleurs, sont ceux qui ont le moins d'inclinaison ; et ceux qui sont tout droits sont préférables, parce k'ils presentent moins de surface au froid dans le tems ou il u plus de force que le soleil, comme en Novembre, Décembre, Janvier, et Février. C'est pour cela que les chassis inclinés, à la façon Hollandoise soit convexes en portion de sfère et dont on recouvre chake partie avec des paillassons à mesure que le soleil les abandone, soit construits en ligne droite, et inclinés, ainsi que le mur sur lekel sont couchés les arbrisseaux à fruits; tels que la vigne, la pêche, &c. qu'on veut avancer, de maniere qu'ils soient perpendiculaires aux raions du soleil au commencement de Mars, ne sont bons que pour ce mois et celui d'Avril, ou le soleil commence à avoir plus de force que les froids des nuits qui diminuent en s'élevant insensiblement au-dessus de la congélation; encore risk t'on en Avril de voir les plantes brûlées en un moment, ou par le moindre coup de soleil lorsk'on ne les ouvre pas, ou par les froids de 7 à 8 deg. lorsk'on les ouvre trop tôt.*" See the whole article entitled *Manière de conserver vivantes dans des serres les plantes des climats les plus chaudes*, tom. i. p. 132.

[2] *Fruit Walls improved by inclining them to the Horizon; or A Way to build Walls for Fruit Trees, whereby they may receive more Sunshine and Heat than ordinary.* By a Member of the Royal Society, London, 1699.

lities which we now possess of protecting sloping walls, and coupled with the information communicated by Dr. Wells[1], may give rise to real improvements.

LAURENCE[2], BRADLEY[3], LONDON and WISE[4], SWITZER[5] and others, have noticed the improvement proposed by M. Facio: but MILLER is the first practical gardener who avowedly treated of the subjects both of inclined walls and sloping glass, with a view to their application to horticultural architecture. He mentions the author of "*Fruit Walls inclined, &c.*" as having "shown by calculation that there will be a much greater number of the sun's rays fall on a wall inclined to the horizon, than on one perpendicular to it;" and of having "taken the trouble of calculating the different inclinations which such walls should have in the different climates, in order to receive the greatest number of the sun's rays." Miller, as is justly remarked by the author of the excellent historical introduction to the "*London Fruit Gardener*," was too apt to condemn his contemporaries, and does not treat Facio with the respect to which he is justly entitled. He condemns the plan with but little argument: and as he was at that time considered in England as the *arbiter olitorum et hortulanorum*, and on the continent as *omnibus in hac arte palmam præripiens*[6], it will readily be conceived that his *ipse dixit* would be sufficient to prevent inclined walls from being tried experimentally. As far as I have been able to ascertain, they were only attempted at Belvoir Castle under Facio's directions. There they were unfortunately built on banks of earth, and found accordingly to be damp, thereby affording Miller a local argument against them, which has been repeated as a funda-

---

[1] *Essay on Dew*, 1814.
[2] *Fruit Garden Kalendar*, 1718. Introduction, pp. 13 and 22.
[3] *New Improvements in Gardening*, art. "Stove;" and in various works by this author from 1700 to 1724.
[4] *London Fruit Gardener*, chapter on Walls.
[5] *Practical Fruit Gardener*, art. Wall.
[6] *Amœnitates Academicæ*, tom. iv. 213.

mental one by almost every writer who has touched on the subject, from his time to the present day; including the compiler of an able article on horticulture just published in the *Edinburgh Encyclopedia* [1].

In the seventh and eighth editions of Miller's Dictionary (the last published in 1768) the articles STOVE, SUN, GREENHOUSE, and several others, are considerably enlarged by reflections and arguments on the slope of glass roofs; in all probability suggested by Facio, Boerhaave, and what the author had seen during his stay in Holland. Speaking of dry stoves, he says they may either be built with "upright and sloping glass" or "with the latter" only "placed at an angle of 45 degrees, the better to admit the rays of the sun in spring and autumn when the sun declines." This he says "has been the general practice;" but he adds, "where I have had the contrivance of stoves of this kind I have always built them after the model of the bark stove (i. e. with upright and sloping glass); because this will the more easily admit the sun at all the different seasons; for in summer when the sun is high, the top glasses will admit the rays to shine almost all over the house, and in winter when the sun is low, the front glasses will admit his rays; whereas when the glasses are laid to any declivity in one direction, the rays of the sun will not fall directly thereon above a fortnight in autumn and about the same time in spring [2]."

We are informed under the article SUN, that as the difference between the heat of summer and winter depends on the obliquity of the sun's rays, this should be well considered in the contrivance of stoves, which ought to have their glasses so situated, as to receive the sun's rays in direct lines, during as great a portion of the year as possible; "for which reason the stoves which have upright glasses in front, and sloping glasses over them, are justly preferred to any at present contrived."

It is proper to remark here, that forcing houses for grapes and

---

[1] Mr. P. Niel, Secretary to the Caledonian Horticultural Society.
[2] Miller's *Dict.* art. Stove.

peaches were less in use in Miller's time, than greenhouses and botanic stoves; and that this author was more a botanical than a culinary gardener. Had the demand among the opulent for early and high-flavoured fruits been as great then as it is now, it is probable so intelligent a writer and general observer would have made a nicer distinction between houses for general purposes, or maintaining an artificial climate during the whole year; and such as are only intended to mature crops of fruit at particular seasons.

The importance of this distinction was reserved to be illustrated by Mr. KNIGHT; who has not only shown its use theoretically, but confirmed its utility by several years experience.

In one of the examples given by Mr. Knight, his object was to force a large and high-flavoured, rather than a very early crop of grapes; and he accordingly fixed upon such a slope, as that the sun's rays might be perpendicular to it in the beginning of July, the period about which he wished the crop to ripen. The slope of the roof to effect this purpose in lat. 52 he of course found to be 34 degrees. The house was forty feet long, with fixed sashes, no front glass, and to which air was admitted at the ends only. It produced, we are informed, "the most abundant crops of grapes perfectly ripened, within less time, and with less expenditure of fuel, than I have witnessed in any other instance[1]."

The second instance of Mr. Knight's application of this principle, is to a peach-house. The sloping glass of this house he placed on an angle of 28 degrees, that the sun's rays might be perpendicular to it *before* the ripening season; because (as peaches ripen with most flavour when exposed to the open air) Mr. K. *removes the lights* before midsummer. This house is fifty feet long, nine feet high, with no

---

[1] *Description of a Forcing-house for Grapes, with Observations on the best Method of constructing them for other Fruits.*—London *Hort. Trans.* vol. i. p. 99.

I had an opportunity of seeing this vinery at Downton Castle, near Ludlow, in the year 1807, shortly after it was built.

front glass, but with the sloping glass moveable to admit air. This plan he recommends, as combining more advantages than can ever be obtained in a higher or wider house. He adds: "I estimate so highly the advantages of bringing forward the fruit under glass till it is nearly full grown, and then exposing it to the stronger stimulus of sunshine, without the intervention of the glass, and excluding it from air and dews, that I believe the peach might be thus ripened in greater perfection at St. Petersburg, in a house properly adapted to the latitude of that place, than in the open air at Rome or Naples." *Hort. Trans.* p. 206.

In addition to these experimental proofs of the excellency of the principle by Mr. Knight, we have a formula for its application, by the Rev. THOMAS WILKINSON [1]. He says: " having determined in what season we wish to have the most powerful effects from the sun, we may construct our houses accordingly, by the following rule. Make the angle contained between the back wall of the house and its roof = to the complement of the latitude of the place ± the sun's declination, for that day on which we wish his rays to fall perpendicularly. From the vernal to the autumnal equinox the declination is to be added, and the contrary."

Mr. Wilkinson has added to his valuable scientific communication Bouguer's [2] Table of rays reflected from glass, which, in connection with the above formula, is extremely useful, and serves to give a striking view of the disadvantages of obliquity to the sun's rays, whatever may be the nature of the surface on which he shines. From this table it appears, that if 1000 rays fall upon a surface of glass at an angle of 75°, 299 of these rays are reflected; consequently in little more than an hour after each mid-day, in spring and autumn, nearly one third of the effect of the sun is lost on all hothouses with parallelogram bases and common sloping roofs fronting the south, what-

---
[1] London *Hort. Trans.* vol. i. p. 161.
[2] See Bouguer, *Traité d'Optique*.

ever may be their angle of inclination; and, that as the sun declines further from the meridian the loss is consequently proportionally great[1].

Before I proceed further in tracing the progress of this principle, I beg leave to refer to the diagrams in PLATE I. which contains an elementary illustration of the whole subject, from 1699 to 1817.

Fig. 1. Is a section of an Orangery, "*according to the laws of Boerhaave:*" it is nearly a fac simile of the diagrams given in the *Encyclopédie Méthodique* and the *Amœnitates Academicæ* under this designation. I mention this, because at first sight it does not appear consistent with the quotation from the *Elementa Chemiæ*, given above, which directs the front glass to be placed at an angle of 14° 30′ "*to the pavement.*" From the context and spirit of the passage, however, we must evidently understand an angle of 14° 30′ to the perpendicular. This diagram may be dated 1720.

Fig. 2. Is a section of the Caldarium or stove erected by Linnæus in the botanic garden at Upsal, in 1740, and referred to by him in his *Descriptio Hortus Upsaliensis* quoted above. It contains horizontal flues (*camini horizontales*) under the front glass and at the ends, for the purpose of heating the house; and in the centre, towards the back wall, an exposed fire-place, or Swedish stove, for drying the internal damps and dispelling exhalations when external air cannot be admitted.

---

[1] The formula for calculating the effects of the sun's rays on opaque surfaces will be found in Facio's work above mentioned, (page 38 *et seq.*) and also in an interesting paper in the *Phil. Trans.* by Dr. Halley, No. 203. The result is, that "the quantity of the sun's rays falling upon any plane, is as the sine of the sun's altitude upon that plane;" and that the force of each ray is governed by the same laws. Whence it follows, "that the whole action of his rays upon a plane is as the square of the sine of the sun's altitude on the plane and the time that action lasts jointly, neglecting the effects of the atmosphere." Coupling this formula with Bouguer's table of rays reflected from glass, it is evident the exact influence of the sun may be calculated on any description of surface, whether transparent or opaque, and however curved or inclined.

Fig. 3. Is the section of what Adanson considers the best form of a greenhouse. The glass being perpendicular, admits the sun's rays in the winter months: it is also less obnoxious to frozen dew, or snow, than sloping houses. In summer the plants are supposed to be placed in the open air.

Fig. 4. Is Adanson's section of a stove or house for general purposes in the neighbourhood of Paris. The ground plan may either be oblong, elliptical, or a tetragon or polygon, similar to the glass. The coincidence of this and some other diagrams given by Adanson, with the semidome proposed by Sir George Mackenzie, is remarkable; and the fact of such houses being common in Holland in Adanson's time, proves that there is but little new at least in this branch of horticulture. These two diagrams may be dated 1760.

Fig. 5. Shows the slope proposed by Nicolas Facio de Douillier for a fruit wall in latitude $52\frac{1}{2}°$. I have shown this wall as placed on arches; but those erected at Belvoir Castle, under Facio's direction, were on banks of earth, as indicated by the dotted lines a, b, c, in this figure. I shall afterwards describe a mode of erecting such walls with a moderate quantity of materials, and of fitting a curtain to them, so as to render them in some degree a medium between a hot-wall and a glass case. Facio's plan is dated 1699.

Fig. 6. Is a design for a Dutch vinery, for the earliest forcing season. The slope of the back wall and that of the glass are nearly alike, a circumstance noted by Adanson in the quotation given from him, and worthy of imitation. The large flues and shed behind of temperate air, to be exchanged with that in the glass case in severe weather, when the external air cannot be admitted, show a degree of care and science beyond what is generally bestowed or discovered in this country. This diagram is nearly a fac simile of one given in the *Encyclopédie Méthodique*. It may be dated 1730.

Fig. 7. Shows the slope of Mr. Knight's vinery.

Fig. 8. The slope of Mr. Knight's peach-house.

Fig. 9. The slope recommended by Miller and the Rev. T. Wilkinson for general purposes, and which seems to be more generally adopted than any other by Mr. Aiton, in the houses constructed under his direction at Kew, Kensington, &c.

Fig. 10. Is the slope for cucumber frames and pits, adopted by Mons. Thouin in the *Jardin des Semis* at Paris[1], and by Mr. Knight in Herefordshire[2].

Fig. 11. Is a vertical section of the glass semidome proposed by Sir George Mackenzie, to be afterwards described.

   a. Situation of the flue which is led round under the glass.
   b. The trellis.
   c. The back wall.

Fig. 12. Is a section of a house designed by Mr. Braddick of the London Horticultural Society, and erected at Mr. Palmer's at Kingston, Surrey. The idea is avowedly taken from Sir George Mackenzie's semidome. Both plan and section are parts of an ellipsis. The sashes open on the principle recommended by Adanson and Mr. Knight, and adopted in the London sky-lights.

   a.   Is the front flue and walk, over which is a wire trellis under the glass for vines.
   b & c. Temporary trellises for peaches, till the vines cover the glass.
   d.   The sashes, as opened to admit air.

Much additional interest has recently attached to the subject of glass roofs, from the plan proposed by Sir GEORGE MACKENZIE; the universal principle of which, together with its elegant appearance, has very naturally fascinated a number of ingenious horticulturists. In 1812 Sir George built a house at Coul, his seat in the Highlands of Scotland, for the production of grapes and peaches, which he describes in the Transactions of the Caledonian Horticultural Society as

---

[1] *Essai sur l'Exposition et la Division méthodique de l'Œconomie rurale,* &c. Paris, 1814.
[2] London *Hort. Trans.* vol. i.

on an improved and œconomical construction[1]; but which he afterwards discovered to be of an opposite description; and with that candour and openness to conviction which is or ought to be the case with

---

[1] The general form of the house was not different from that of common oblong houses, with sloping glass. The improvements consisted in having no front or end glass; the sloping glass fixed with a trellis under it for vines, and with transverse trellises for peaches. These transverse trellises were formed in the original plan of open work in the usual way; but in any future house built on this principle, transverse brick walls were intended to be substituted, as better adapted to retain the heat. The object gained was nearly double the extent of trellis, and a greater command of temperature; from which of course was expected more fruit, at less expense. It strikes me as somewhat remarkable, that this plan found its way into the Transactions of a society composed chiefly of practical men; since any gardener could have predicted its failure; and it does not appear to merit being recorded, from any general reasoning calculated to excite new ideas. Besides, cross trellises had been already tried in Scotland, at Sir John Stewart's, near Lanark.

I hope I shall not be suspected of enlarging on this subject from any adverse feeling towards Sir G. Mackenzie, for whom I have a very high respect. I state the fact entirely for the sake of proving to my readers, that though the Transactions of these societies abound in valuable communications, yet that every plan introduced, however plausibly recommended, must not be implicitly followed, or considered as at once setting at nought old practices; nor every result, however interesting or partially known, considered as a new discovery. Having adduced an instance in support of the former, I shall prolong this note by adding one to illustrate the latter proposition.

Fruit trees are apt very frequently to become too luxuriant in branches and foliage, and to produce but few blossoms. It is, therefore, a most desirable object to counteract this tendency; and in the papers of both societies the results of various attempts are given, attended with different degrees of success; to almost each of which the inexperienced reader would be apt to award the palm due to original discovery. One gardener lays bare their roots during the winter season; another during the summer months; and both find more blossom produced the following year. Another cuts off part of the main roots; a fourth saws the main stems of his trees half through; a fifth bends down the extremities of the branches, or puts a cincture of wire round them where they issue from the main stem or leader. Each of these modes, as well as several others, will be attended more or less with the desired effect; and to render any one of them known to such as are ignorant of the whole, though it be of importance, need not be mistaken for originality. The fact is, the success of all the modes depends on one simple principle known and practised before the time of Vitruvius or Virgil, and consists in preventing the main body of the cortical sap, while in action in the branches, from returning to reinvigorate the roots. It has always been known to physiologists and to many scientific gar-

every one who attempts to devise or introduce improvement, and which may be said to be characteristic of Sir George Mackenzie, he was the first to notice the mistake he had fallen into[1].

The failure or disapprobation of this plan would, no doubt, lead the active and philosophic mind of its author to take a more scientific view of the subject; and, in as far as respects the principle of perpendicularity to the sun's rays, he seems to have been particularly happy in reaping the fruit of all his contemporaries in that department of construction. For, by going one step further than they have done, he has hit on the ultimatum of the principle.

Every reader who is in the habit of seeing the London Horticultural Society's Transactions will be aware that I allude to a paper in their second volume, entitled " On the form which the glass of a forcing-house ought to have, in order to receive the greatest possible quantity of rays from the sun: by Sir George Mackenzie, bart. F.R.S. read August 1, 1815."

In this paper Sir George observes, that he does not presume that any of the members of the *London* Horticultural Society are ignorant of the solution of so simple a problem as " what that figure is which will receive the greatest possible quantity of the sun's rays at all times of the day, and at all seasons of the year." " That form," he then observes, " is to be found in the sphere; and it is the segment of a globe which I propose for the glass, when it is desired to receive into a forcing-house the greatest possible quantity of light. The segment is one fourth, or a semidome, which I consider as sufficient, though to

---

deners, and is best performed by cutting off a circle of bark round each branch when the tree is in blossom. Buffon tried this practice both on fruit and forest trees, in the year 1733, with great success, and has given an account of his experiments in the *Mémoires de l'Académie des Sciences*, A. D. 1788. See also a general history and rationale of the practice in the *Journal Physico-Œconomique*, communicated by Mons. Suriray Delarue, 1803; Darwin's *Phytologia*, vol. i. p. 393; and *Botanic Garden*, vol. i. canto 4; and various other authors, as Hales, Grew, Adanson, &c.

[1] Introductory remarks to the paper on the Semidome. London *HortTrans*. vol. ii.

catch the sun at all times during summer the segment would have to correspond with the greatest circle which the sun describes."

The plan and elevation given are next described.

The plan is a semicircle, the diameter a back wall. The elevation a semidome of glass, placed on a low front wall. The entrance is in the back wall, or rather in a sort of porch to a recess in that wall, against which recess the trellis is placed. Air is proposed to be admitted by openings in the front wall, and at the top of the back wall; or, it is added in a postscript, " by making the glass semidome in two parts, and placing it on rollers, in the manner of an observatory dome, the whole might be moved with great ease and safety, so as to expose the plants in the interior to the direct influence of the sun, &c."

The author of the article "Horticulture" in the *Edinburgh Encyclopædia* has introduced this plan among the recent improvements in hothouses, of which he has a very favourable idea; and adds, " Mr. Knight, we understand, highly approves of this invention, and is of opinion that it will answer every purpose *better than any form hitherto contrived*."

Whilst I cordially agree with the writer of the article alluded to, as to the elegance of the plan, and consider it in many respects a desirable addition to horticultural architecture, I certainly must dissent from the opinion stated (doubtless from good authority) to be that of Mr. Knight. So far from thinking it fit for every purpose, I am persuaded that it cannot be so successfully and œconomically applied to the forcing department as the best plans now in use. Whether my reasons are well grounded, must be left for the reader and future experience to determine. There can be little harm in submitting them if the plan is really " *better than any form hitherto contrived*," while if to some its advantages appear doubtful, discussion may tend to remove those doubts.

Figs. 1 and 2, (Pl. II.) may be considered as an outline of the ground plan and elevation; and *Fig.* 11 of Pl. I. as a section of this design. Though mere dimension has little to do with the properties of any figure, yet I shall in examining the semidome adopt those given by its author. The diameter or length of the ground plan is thirty feet; and its radius, or height and width, fifteen feet. The trellis being placed against the back wall, is, of course, the greatest vertical section contained in the figure. Now, if the sun had an equally great effect upon the earth's surface, during every moment which he appears above our horizon; and if his influence on plants in a glass case were equally great when they are ten or fifteen feet, as when they are two or three feet from the glass, then would this design be unexceptionable, as far as respected the *attainment of one object in view*. But we are taught by experience that the horizontal rays of the rising and setting sun, from their obliquity, as well as from the mist and vapours through which they have to pass, have but little effect; and that the most vivid of his rays which at any hour of the day pervade a window or a hothouse, become so divergent a few feet within the glass as to produce attenuation in young plants, and to lose great part of their influence in ripening fruits. As therefore a large portion of the glass in this design depends for its effect on the morning and evening sun, and as great part of the trellis will be from five to fifteen feet from the glass, its disadvantages will be at once sufficiently obvious to practical men.—It will receive but few and weak rays in the morning and evening, and what enters the glass in the middle part of the day will be too far from the trees.

On inspecting *Fig.* 1. the elevation of the trellis, it will appear that there is a circumferential portion of it, $k, k, k,$ which at all events is not far distant from the glass; and a superficial observer would conclude that on this part of the house every advantage of the sun's rays would be obtained. But though this semiring, as it may be called, be nearer the open air or reflected light, than any other portion of the trellis, yet, from the figure of the house, it will receive least benefit from the sun's rays, for the following reasons:

1. As every line falling perpendicularly on the surface of a circle must be parallel to its axis; consequently, on whatever part of the

semidome the sun's rays fall perpendicular to the glass, they must tend to the centre of the house, which lies of course at an equal distance from every part of the glass at the bottom of the back wall, viz. at *n* in *Fig.* 1 and 2. Therefore his influence on any other part of the trellis must always be inversely as the distance of that part from the centre.

2. As the quantity of heat and light produced by the sun's rays is as the squares of the sines of the angles of their elevation, it follows that his minimum of influence for each day is at his greatest declination; that is, at morning and evening. Therefore, when this circumferential portion of the trellis does enjoy the direct influence of the sun, it enjoys his least possible direct influence.

3. The maximum of the sun's influence will be at midday, when he is perpendicular to the central part of the glass dome (as at *I*, *Fig.* 1 and 2). But when his rays are most perpendicular to his centre, they are most oblique to his sides. Therefore, when the sun has most power in communicating his influence, the circumferential part of the trellis has the least means of receiving it.

Ocular demonstration may be obtained to the same effect by inspecting the dotted lines in the figures. If *a*, *b*, *c*, in both diagrams represent the sun's path in the heavens on any particular day,—say on the 22d of June,—then *a* will represent sunrise, *b* midday, and *c* sunset.

Hence the sun having advanced eighteen degrees in his diurnal course, or to *E*, his rays fall perpendicularly on the glass at *e*. At *e* 2 the angle of incidence is 8°, at *e* 3 it is 7°, and at *e* 4 it is 10°; consequently, according to Bouguer's table of rays, at each of these places 25 rays in every 1000 are reflected.

Advanced 36 degrees, or to *F*, his rays fall perpendicularly at *f*: at *f* 2 the angle of incidence is 6°, at *f* 3, 12°, at *f* 4, 17°, and at each of these points the same proportion of rays as above is reflected.

Advanced 72 degrees, or to *H*, his rays fall perpendicularly at *h*. At *h* 2 the angle of incidence is 9°, at *h* 3, 19°, and at *h* 4, 29°: at

(19)

the two former points 25, and at the latter 27, rays in 1000 are reflected.

Advanced 90 degrees, or to his meridian at I, his rays fall perpendicularly at b. At i 2 and 3, 25 rays, and at i 4, 27 rays, in 1000 are reflected.

In this way an accurate estimate may be formed of the proportionate number of the sun's rays which fall on different parts of the trellis; and the absolute force of these rays may be similarly estimated from the dotted lines answering to the same letters in *Fig.* 1, which indicate the sun's altitude; leaving always out of the question atmospherical, dioptrical, and other accidental effects[1]. The conclusion is obviously what I first stated on general grounds; that the circumference of the trellis will not have sufficient solar influence, and that the central part will be too far from the glass, the intermediate spaces partaking of course of the two extremes. Therefore it does not appear to me *the best plan hitherto devised for ripening fruit*.

The radius of the semidome being fifteen feet, the contents of the trellis will be 353.42 feet; and of the semidome of glass 706.84 feet. Now in a common oblong house, with the trellis about eleven inches from the glass, a superficies of trellis is obtainable equal to that of the glass. Here it is considerably under one half of the glass's surface; so that in respect to expense of glass roofing, the difference between a common house and the semidome is as two to one against the latter.

The mass of air to be heated by one fire will be 353.858 cubic feet;

---

[1] As many persons are not practically aware of the astonishing difference between the effects of the sun when perpendicular, and when oblique, to a transparent surface, I would suggest the simple experiment of placing a pane of glass between that luminary and the eye, and giving it different degrees of obliquity. By observing his effects also at different hours of the day in the large bell glasses used for protecting cucumbers, some idea may be formed of his operation on a dome. Divide one of these glasses vertically by a board covered with white paper. Wash this paper with muriate of silver and expose it to the south, similarly to the back wall of the semidome. The deoxidising rays will take effect, and after some weeks that part of the paper on which the sun has had most influence will be the blackest.

giving 353.42 feet of trellis. But a house forty feet by twelve, and twelve high, contains 2880 cubic feet also to be heated by one moderate fire, and gives 660 superficial feet of trellis. Here the calculation is still greater against this design: so that on the whole it does not seem *the best plan hitherto devised in point of œconomy.*

Something would be gained for this figure by imagining the trellis of the same form as the glass, and placed eleven or twelve inches within it. The contents of the trellis would be increased, and the vaulted canopy of fruit and foliage in the ripening season would be most elegant; but one half of the trellis would be in shade great part of the morning, and the other half great part of the afternoon. At midday no part would be under shade; yet then the obliquity of the sun's rays to the sides of the dome would exclude a considerable circumferential space next the back wall from their direct effects.

Joined to a vertical trellis, there might be a horizontal one, which would double the extent of space for training. But the objections to a vertical trellis apply with equal force to a horizontal one; and unless mere *quantity* of fruit, without regard to *quality*, were the object, this plan is not to be recommended.

Probably the best form of a trellis would be that of a flattened semidome, or segment of an oblate spheroid, whose boundary lines should coincide with those of the glass, and whose lesser axis of the elliptic base should not exceed two thirds of the axis of the dome. *Fig.* 3, Pl. II. is a horizontal section of such a trellis. When, however, we compare, in imagination, the sun at midday perpendicular to one spot of a glass semidome, and the sun's rays at midday passing perpendicularly through every pane of a common sloping roof, properly adjusted to the ripening season, and exercising their full influence on the crop of fruit spread out immediately under the glass, the difference is striking, and decisively against the semidome as a *forcing-house.*

As fruits to be ripened in perfection must be kept very near the glass, a much better form than a semidome is a segment of a circle, frequently employed by the Dutch, and of which an instance may be seen in a vinery built by the late Mr. Hope of East Sheen[1]. A portion of an ellipsis, also in use among the Dutch, is still better, and has recently been adopted by Mr. Palmer at his villa at Kingston[1], as suggested by an active member of the Horticultural Society, Mr. Braddick of Thames Ditton[1].

Fig. 4, Pl. II. is an outline of the ground plan of Mr. Hope's vinery; and *Fig.* 5 of that of Mr. Palmer;—both from memory.

But though the semidome cannot be adopted as a forcing-house without considerable disadvantages, yet it may be used in some cases even for maturing fruits; and as its appearance is most elegant, and it admits of a happy combination of lightness with strength in the construction; it may be considered, with the improvements of which it is susceptible, as a most valuable acquisition to the horticultural architecture of this country. For greenhouses, conservatories, and every description of botanical hothouse, it is indeed peculiarly applicable.

As an improvement, I should propose in *all cases* to acuminate its apex, the better to throw off the rain; and in *some cases* to spread out its base (thus giving it a campanulate form), in order to admit of small plants being placed close under the glass.

In most cases, however, I should prefer an entire and detached dome, or acuminated solid of revolution of glass on all sides, to a semidome, as a more elegant single object, and as admitting light in every direction. A large conservatory on this plan attached to the mansion, or a greenhouse placed in the centre of a small lawn in a flower-garden or shrubbery, would be more elegant, as well as more congenial to the plants, than the present square or triangular shed-like buildings placed against walls.

On a moderate scale—say twenty or thirty feet diameter—they are admirably adapted for receiving exotic Floras; as for the Erica, New

---

[1] Surrey.

Holland, Cape, Palm, Chinese, or Succulent tribes. On a large scale, they would admit of the growth of trees almost to their natural size; as for example, the Norfolk Island Pine, Musa, &c. in the centre, and smaller growths towards the circumference: and by a little judicious contrivance they might be constructed low at first, and raised according to the progress of the trees.

PLATE III. contains a section of a campanulated house, fifty feet high, intended for large trees in the centre, and smaller articles towards the circumference.

    a. The flues, and pathway over.
    b. Mode of opening the whole of the glass to admit at pleasure air, wind, rain, and the direct influence of the sun.
    c. Basement walls.

Fig. 1, PL. IV. is an elevation of an acuminated figure, intended as a small dry stove. The glass, excepting the acuminated part, is fixed; air being admitted by raising that part of the glass, and by opening the horizontal shutters in the basement wall.

Fig. 2. is a vertical section, in which the acuminated part is shown raised to admit air. Under the pavement of the circular walk is a can flue bedded in dry sand, as seen at *a*. Under the stage, *b, b*; which is a cone of steps, is a reservoir, *c*, into which the flue, after having made the circuit of the house, discharges itself; thus affording the smoke ample space to give out its caloric, before it escapes by the horizontal chimney, *d*. By casing each step with a thin circular band of plate iron, a cone of earth or bark might be formed, and thus a moist heat supplied; or a common circular bark pit might be substituted for the stage and reservoir, &c.

Fig. 3 is a plan, and *Fig.* 4 a dissected vertical profile, showing the arrangement of the astragals of the roof, and the walk, basement wall, entrance, &c. Elegance being a principal consideration in buildings of this sort, it is almost needless to mention that the fire-place, chimney-top, &c. should be properly concealed, which in general can be readily effected by bushes, or other local facilities.

In PLATE V. *Fig.* 1, a design is submitted, in which a part of the idea suggested by Adanson and Sir George Mackenzie is applied to what I would call a *forcing-house for general purposes*, as opposed to such as are calculated for particular seasons, and for ripening the whole crop at once, which takes place in common houses with inclined roofs, and may be very suitable for an immense establishment, but is not to be desired where there are perhaps but one or two houses for each department. To the idea of a semidome or curved roof I have added one of my own; and though I have not hitherto had an opportunity of executing it on a large scale, yet it is evidently well calculated to promote the influence of the sun on the trellis of every description of longitudinal house. I allude to what I call a ridge and furrow disposition of the glass, which is to be effected in two ways, viz. either by *ridge and furrow glazing*, or by *ridge and furrow roofing*.

In the first, instead of having the astragals of a sash in the same plane, they are placed in two planes alternately, raising one and depressing the other; so that, when glazed, the glass declines from the high or ridge astragal, to the low or furrow astragal. The cross section of a sash so glazed would be a zig-zag line, as in *Fig.* 1, PLATE VI.

Ridge and furrow roofing is merely effecting the same object on a larger scale, by raising and depressing the rafters alternately, as shown in the section *Fig.* 2, PLATE VI.

The object to be attained by this mode of glazing is *two daily meridians*; the one earlier, and the other later than the natural meridian, in proportion to the angle of elevation of the ridge astragals or rafters. In this way the sun's perpendicular influence is obtained an hour or two earlier, and retained an hour or two later, all over the house; an object which in longitudinal houses facing the south cannot be effected by any other means. This proposed improvement applies equally to front as to sloping glass, and whether the slope be rectilineal, or part of a circle, polygon, or other figure. Domes, and houses whose plans are segments of circles or of ellipses, are those only to which it does not offer any, or but few advantages.

Imagine *Fig.* 1, PL. VI. to be a section of a sash glazed in the ridge and furrow manner; *Fig.* 2 a section of a common sash; and a, b, c, in both figures, the sun's course. Then, when the sun arrives at a, or eleven o'clock, in *Fig.* 1, he is perpendicular to one half of the glass of the sash; but when at a, *Fig.* 2, his rays form an angle of 72° with its surface; and the incidental angle being 20°, 25 rays in every 1000 are reflected. In like manner in the afternoon, when he arrives at one o'clock, the same advantages will result to *Fig.* 1, and the same disadvantages to *Fig.* 2; and this, whether the sashes are placed in an upright or in a sloping direction.

It is true there is a corresponding loss of 25° in 1000 when the sun is at b, or in the natural meridian: but as each ray, from being then at its greatest elevation, has its maximum of power, the loss sustained will be more than counterbalanced by the earlier and later meridians, which give a double chance of obtaining the sun's full influence in cloudy weather, and prolong his influence in clear weather.

There is another advantage of the ridge and furrow glazing shown in *Fig.* 1, which will be found of consequence in hotbeds, pits, and in all flat roofs of glass. When the declivity from the ridge astragal to the furrow astragal is greater than the slope of the roof, the internal dews will of course be thrown towards the furrow astragal. By forming a gutter, d, *Fig.* 1, on the under edge of the moulding of that astragal, these dews may be collected and carried off; and in this way, *dropping*, so much complained of by gardeners in early cucumber frames, and in most houses with a glazed lap or overlap, may be more effectually prevented than by any other mode hitherto devised. I have proved this in a greenhouse and pit erected here, in which one sash glazed in the ridge and furrow manner is placed in the same roof with six others glazed in as many different modes, and all at an angle of 11 degrees. As they are very flat, some drops fall from the whole of them; but invariably the smallest number from the ridge and furrow sash, and in the proportion of one to five with the close puttied, or closed metallic lap.

Fig. 3 is a section of part of a ridge and furrow roof, which on inspection will be found to be merely a disposition of sashes, similarly to the disposition of panes in Fig. 1, and consequently that it produces the same effects. In this mode it is necessary that the slope of the roof be greater than the slope from the ridge rafter, d, to the furrow rafter, e, in order that neither the inside dews nor the rains externally may rest on the puttied rabbets of the astragals. Such a house as that of which Pl. I. Fig. 6. is a section, would be rendered complete as the earliest description of forcing-house, by having its glasses disposed in this manner, and at such an angle as that the early meridian might take place at ten, and the late at two o'clock.

But to return to the design submitted in Pl. V.—Here are no rafters; but a curved astragal, with the upper part straight, is used throughout, and only supported or steadied by two horizontal cross bars of the same thickness as the astragals. The ends are quarter domes, glazed as in the hemispherical house. The whole roof is fixed, air being admitted by the horizontal shutters in the front wall, and the windows at top and bottom of the back wall. The longitudinal part of the roof between the two ends, though presenting as a whole a convex surface, yet in detail is ribbed or glazed in the ridge and furrow manner just described. A canvass outer roofing is adapted to the glass. The results of this construction are—

1. From the globular form of the longitudinal part as a whole, the sun will be perpendicular to some part of it every midday throughout the year.

2. From the ridge and furrow glazing of its detail, he will be perpendicular to half the entire roof twice in every day throughout the year.

3. From the use of astragals without uprights, imposts, rafters, sashes, &c. &c. and from the circular ends, the greatest possible quan-

tity of transparent surface is obtained consistently with a moderate size of panes.

4. The canvass covering, by preserving a heated atmosphere outside the glass, will retain the heat within, prevent dews from condensing, or water-drops from forming on the glass, and lessen the consumption of fuel, as well as the risk from too great or too little heat during night.

Contrast this construction with any form hitherto devised;—with the common sloping roof, to which the sun cannot be perpendicular more than twice a year, and where a third of his rays are obstructed by rafters, sash-frames, &c.; with the globular house or semidome, where the trellis is too far from the glass; with the roof at an elevated angle, which loses great part of the sun's effects at midsummer; and with that at a depressed angle, which loses great part of his effects in midwinter;—and the advantages of this house will appear striking. That it will be less expensive in the erection, must be evident from the entire omission of rafters and moveable lights. The following detail will render this design more intelligible:

In *Figs.* 1, 2, and 3,

- *a.* represents the foundation piers of the front wall.
- *b.* Air valves, or shutters between each pier.
- *c.* Coping of the front wall, showing a plan of the zig-zag or ridge and furrow glazing.
- *d.* The quarter dome ends and entrance doors.
- *e.* Front trellis.
- *f.* Trellis for temporary use, placed in the back part of the house, and inclined towards the back wall.
- *g.* Front flue.
- *h.* Course of flue in back shed to temperate the air for the growth of mushrooms, and for ventilating the front house.
- *i.* Windows for the purposes of ventilation and light to mushroom-house and sheds.

k. Two rooms, in which are the furnaces, but which may be also used for potting or shifting plants, &c. or fitted up as seed- or fruit-rooms.

r. Glass division, in order to admit of different management or original disposition in respect to the fruits to be forced.

s. Rolls of canvass, which form the outer roofing, and are let down and drawn up in the manner of common linen window blinds. The ends are covered by gores of canvass, rolled up under the coping of the front wall, and drawn to the apex, on the same principle as the others are let down.

The same slope of glass adopted in this design is of course applicable to any dimension or description of house; to various modes of opening the glasses for air, and arranging the trellis, flues, back wall, &c. To illustrate this I shall give the outlines of five different modes, answering to the five remaining sections in PLATE V.

In *Fig.* 4. iron rafters are fixed six or eight feet asunder, and iron frames of such a length as to reach from centre to centre of the rafters, and three or three feet and half broad, are placed on them, and attached to the rafters by hinges at the upper angles. The astragals are placed in the direction of the breadth, not of the length, of these frames; and the styles either formed to the curve of the roof, or the curve reduced to part of a polygon, whose sides are each three feet and half. This arrangement properly completed, then by means of levers attached to each frame, either inside or outside the house, the whole roof may be raised, either to the perpendicular to admit a shower, or to any required angle, according to the sun's altitude at the hour of the day and season of the year. The detail of the construction requisite for this operation is given in PLATE VII. which will be afterwards referred to.

a. (in *Fig.* 4.) represents the levers.

b. The cord attached to them.

c. The situation of the sashes, raised at an angle to admit the sun at midsummer to every part of the house.

d. The situation of the sashes, raised perpendicularly or to the greatest required elevation, so as to admit a shower of rain.

e. Front trellis, with intervals of two feet opposite the centre of each sash.

f. Secondary trellis [1], two feet behind the other, for temporary purposes, or laying back barren wood from the principal trellis.

g. Flue.

h. Pathway.

i. Openings for ventilation, &c.

k. Canvass roofing.

In *Fig.* 5. there is no perpendicular back wall, but the glass and trellis are placed on the south side of a longitudinal arch or vault of brickwork. The glass is divided into two parts; the first, composing two-thirds of the whole slope, consists of astragals without rafters, their lower ends placed ridge and furrow ways on the coping of the front wall, but their upper ends terminating in one plane on a horizontal bearing bar, represented by *a*. The remaining third of the glass is intended to open, and consists of frames glazed in the common mode, hinged at the upper edge, and resting by the lower on the above horizontal bar. These frames are raised by means of a lever, &c. as in the last example.

a. The horizontal bearing bar with supports.

b b. Valves for ventilation, and which, from their situation and the effect of the sun in heating the narrow volume of air between the glass and the brickwork, will be sufficient to lower the house to the temperature of the open air in the hottest day of summer.

c. Valve for admitting heated air from

d, which may either be a receptacle for the smoke after it has made the transit of the front flue, or it may be used as a

---

[1] See Nicol; also Henderson in Niel, "on Scottish Gardens and Orchards," in the *General Report on Scotland*, &c. chap. ix.

place of fermentation for short grass, weeds, dung, tan, &c. the heated air from which may, at certain seasons, be let into the house; or it may be used for both purposes; or for steam; or merely as a reservoir of temperate air, to be interchanged as occasion may require.

e. Front trellis.
f. Back ditto.
g. Outer curtain or roofing.

Fig. 6. Here the glass roof, trellises, and mode of ventilation, are in all respects the same as in the last figure; but instead of a whole, there is only a half vault, resting on cross parapets, and abutting against the upper part of the back wall. It is therefore a variation of *Fig.* 5. adapted to gardens where the walls are already built. The ground plan of the cross walls, and the manner in which this half vault is to be built, will be understood from inspecting *Fig.* 4, Pl. VI. in which

a. represents the piers of the arches of the cross bearing walls.
b. The foundation of the connected segments of the semivault.
c. The back wall.

In *Fig.* 7, Pl. V., is shown the mode of adapting the fruiting-pit of a pinery to this description of roof. The inclination of the bark-bed is parallel to that of the roof; but as tan, leaves, or dung, will not subside in such a position with sufficient regularity to keep the pots upright, deal boards may be placed on edge in the bark, lengthways of the house, and with their upper edges arranged to the required section, and so as to retain level each row of pots. Another mode is to place a cast iron frame or netting on the surface of the bark-bed, having holes or rings for holding the pots, and so contrived as to sink as the bed sinks. By either of these modes the plants will be kept upright, and at an equal distance from the glass.

The reader need not be told the reason why those plants which are intended to fruit in November, December, January, and February, are to be placed in the first and second rows; those in March and April, in the third; May and June, in the fourth; and so on.

(30)

Where neither leaves nor bark are used, but the plants merely plunged in rotted dung or earth[1], or where bottom heat is supplied by steam[2], no boards or frame will be requisite; and in these cases the superiority of this style of roof will be obvious.

a ... b. Section of the cast iron frame for retaining the pots.
c. Walks and flues under.
d. Bark-pit.
e. Vault under.
f. Steaming-pipe for bottom heat.
g. Branches from the steaming-pipe for steaming the air of the house.
h. Back shed and reservoir of air for the purposes of ventilation.
i. Openings for the same purpose.

Fig. 5, Pl. VI. is a plan of the cast iron framing, which may be cast in pieces to be joined by hose at a, a, a, &c.

This construction is calculated to remove a very great objection to the best modern pineries, which is, the obliquity of both the glass and the pit to the sun's rays in the winter season. In some of the best pineries the sloping glass is placed at an angle of 20 degrees, and the pit in which the plants are plunged is level. By this means not only a large proportion of the incident rays are reflected off the glass, but those which enter are oblique to the plants. If there is front glass, the sun will enter it with more effect; but the plants being on a level, the degree of obliquity at which his rays fall on them is as great or greater than before[3].

---

[1] Pines planted on a bank of earth in a glass case constructed from my plans, were grown with great success at Underley Park, near Kendall, Westmoreland, the seat of Alexander Nowell, esq. from 1809 to 1811.—I have not since heard from that quarter, but have no reason to believe they are not still in a thriving state.

[2] For instances of this see "*A short Treatise on Hothouses,*" Edin. 1805, by the author of these Remarks.

[3] In a pinery which I have lately erected in South Wales, I have, besides adapting the slope

Fig. 8. Here the same description of glass roof is shown, as placed against the south side of a gardener's house or row of cottages, and the air to be heated by their fires. This is readily accomplished, either by raising the flues two feet higher than usual, or by lowering the floor of the cottages relatively to that of the house.

The roof of the cottage may either be constructed of timber and tiled in the usual manner, or for durability it may be of arched masonry. In this last case, as a nine-inch brick wall would be too slight, and as a fourteen-inch wall would require such a quantity of bricks as to occasion considerable expense, these three methods may be substituted for a common roof:—

1. *Cross walls*, as in *Fig.* 4, Pl. VI., but at such a distance as to form one apartment between each, may be adopted, with the lateral arched walls of nine instead of four inches.

2. *Cast iron rafters*, with flanches, may be substituted for these cross walls, and double the number used; in which case a four-inch lateral arch will be sufficiently strong. *Fig.* 7, Pl. VI. shows a plan of part of these lateral arches, abutting on the ribs.

   a. The ribs of cast iron.
   b. Wrought iron rods, which tie them together.
   c. Segments which form the lateral arches.

3. *One large arch* may be used, forming the brickwork, so as the section of a fourteen-inch wall may be in fact a zig-zag four-inch wall, as in *Fig.* 6, Pl. VI. I have proved this[1] to be equally strong as a fourteen-inch wall, while it does not consume many more than one third of the bricks. It would also, in all the seven designs which have been described, correspond admirably with the intention of the ridge and furrow glazing; since, when the sun's rays were perpendi-

---

of the pit to that of the sloping glass, contrived a stage immediately adjoining the front glass, on which to place pines coming into fruit during the winter months, for their greater enjoyment of the sun's rays, without which there can be no flavour in fruits.

[1] In a garden wall erected here (Bayswater), 125 feet long and 8 feet high, the upper part of which is merely brick on edge, and all the rest four-inch work, or brick on bed.

cular to half the glass in the early meridian, he would at the same time be perpendicular to half the wall or arch behind the trellis. It is in some degree foreign to the present work to introduce the subject of garden walls; but I may be allowed to remark, that by fixing a proper trellis to the zig-zag wall, so as to form one line or plane with the general front of the masonry, this style of walling would be much better adapted for training fruit-trees in gardens than that in common use, whilst the cost would be little more than one third of a solid fourteen-inch wall. But of this *plus ultra*.

I have now to give the detail of what I consider to be the best mode of opening the sashes of glass houses, referred to above, in the description of *Fig.* 4.

Raising the sashes I consider with Mr. Knight as greatly superior to arrangements in which they slide over or pass each other; for the part of the house beneath or next the double glass is deprived of half its usual quantity of sun and light; and besides, in this way the plants can never enjoy the benefit of a shower. In many pineries, and other wide houses, the upper sashes let down, and the under ones draw up; and when this is done, the consequence is, that in the middle part of the roof over the pit the glass is double, and the plants are darkened, whilst the sun's rays are only admitted directly where they are useless, viz. to the path at the back and front of the house.

Fig. 2, Pl. VII. represents a rafter, on which are placed five sashes of equal dimensions, the one overlapping the other, and each hinged at the upper angle.

    a. a. are levers which may be attached in various ways to a central bar, or to one of the side bars in each sash, or to each side bar if the sash is broad.

    a. b. c. The circle in which the point, *a*, of this lever moves.

It will be sufficiently evident that by attaching a cord to the end of any one lever, and passing that cord over a pulley attached to the under edge of the rafter, the sash may be raised after the manner of common sky-lights, as suggested by Adanson's diagram, *Fig.* 3, Pl. I, but this would be a clumsy mode for so many sashes, and would occupy too much time. The problem therefore is, how to move the whole so as to elevate and retain them at any required angle?

This is to be solved by passing a cord, wire, or chain, d, through the ends of all the levers, with stops on the cords at e, e, e, in order that when the cord is pulled by hand or otherwise at f, the sashes 1, 2, 3, 4, may be raised to g, i.e. to the angle of sash 5 before that sash is moved. The moment that sash moves, then the whole range are in the same plane or angle, g, and may be further elevated to any degree; as for example to 63°, represented by h, for the greatest altitude of the sun near London; or to i, the perpendicular for the admission of rain. When the sashes are to be let down, the upper one, 5, will shut first, and the rest in order; while the stop k will remain at a, k, and the cord will rest in a sort of parabolic curve between the ends e, e, of the levers. The power at f may be a screw wheel, working in a pinion having a small cylinder on which the cord winds up, as represented by *Fig.* 4. The levers and stops may be arranged after the manner of *Fig.* 5; the stop a in that figure being represented with a small screw to attach it to any part of the cord at pleasure; and by which means, if thought desirable, variations may be made in the opening of the sashes. For instance, by fixing the stop of $e, 5$, at a, k, sashes 1 and 5, which are in the most sheltered parts of the roof, may be raised in severe weather for the admission of a little air, and the rest, which are in the most exposed part, kept shut to exclude the storm.

Fig. 1 is merely a variation of the same mode, in which the sashes are hinged, or turn on pivots, at or near their centres. Of course this mode will not answer where vines or other trees are trained near (that is within two feet of) the glass; but for lofty botanic houses (such as that delineated in PL. IV.) it is to be preferred to any other; as, from one half of each sash nearly balancing the other, little power is required to elevate them; while their pivots are still so far removed from the centre of each sash towards its upper angle, as to lower them by their own gravity, and hold them down. This effect is further aided by the weights shown depending from the extremities of the cords in the apex of the section in Pl. IV.

For Mr. Angerstein's greenhouse, the large conservatory at Stockholm, or those immense stoves erected at Schönbrun; or for such as I have heard the Prince Regent intends to erect at Brighton, and, as Sir Joseph Banks predicts, will hereafter be erected generally in this country to admit the full growth of exotic trees; this plan is peculiarly adapted. Indeed there seems hardly any other way that such houses could be so arranged as to give the trees in their earlier years, and during their progress from the floor to the roof, any chance of growing to that height in a healthy state; for, admitting them to be regularly supplied with light, heat, air, and water; yet that tree could hardly support itself long, which had attained the height of 50 feet, without deriving the advantages, which Mr. Knight has so ably proved are derivable, from wind. Sir Joseph suggests that such houses may be heated by steam; and I may add, that on the boilers used for this purpose, machinery connected with a thermometer on Mr. Kewley's plan, might be contrived to open and shut the sashes of these immense roofs almost instantaneously [1].

An objection will be urged against circular or curved roofs, from the greater expense of all curved work, compared with that in which straight lines prevail. This would be an argument of considerable force, if it were proposed to have either the rafters or astragals of timber; and if, in addition to this, uprights, imposts, sliding sashes, &c. were necessary. But as great part of these roofs are composed of astragals only, without rafters, the objection is of trifling weight. The expense of such roofs as *Figs.* 3, 5, 6, 7, and 8, Pl. V. will be little more than if they were of one declination or inclined plane. The whole business of iron roofs and sashes, and particularly of iron astra-

---

[1] A fine specimen of what may be done with cast iron rafters, in curved roofs, may be seen in Brown and Co.'s chain cable manufactory, Isle of Dogs.

gals, will be materially simplified and improved by the introduction of solid iron astragals. These I have prevailed on an eminent iron-master to attempt, by drawing rods of iron through suitable moulds; and after repeated trials, at considerable expense, he has at last succeeded in producing an article, which, if the expression be not too high for the subject, will form a new æra in sash-making. Hitherto metallic astragals have been formed of two or more pieces, the moulding and rabbet apart, and the latter let into a groove in the former, or in some instances only soldered to it. To bend such astragals to a curved line is with some sorts impossible, and with every description must evidently lessen their strength; but with a solid body the case is materially different: by heating a solid iron astragal it may be bent to any shape whatever, and yet retain all its original tenacity; and if the convex side of the curve is placed uppermost, as in the case of these roofs, it is evident the astragal will be much stronger than if retained in a straight direction.

But the grand advantage of metallic astragals and iron rafters in glass roofs, is the increase thereby obtained of transparent surface. No person intending to construct a house, and who values the *quality* of fruit, ought ever to hesitate as to their adoption. If mere quantity is the object, a common wooden house will answer every purpose; but where the expense of a glass case is incurred, it will always be found the wisest œconomy to have one, all other circumstances being equal, which admits the greatest possible quantity of light.

That the operation of different constructions may be judged of in this respect, I shall here estimate the quantity of transparent surface in six different descriptions of roof, taking the roof of *Fig.* 1, Pl. V. as the most transparent; and the best constructed wooden houses; such, for example, as those of Kensington Gardens and Kew, as the minimum of my scale.

In each of these examples I imagine the house to be forty feet long, and twelve feet wide, with a front wall one foot high, the front glass two feet (where front glass is used), and the back wall fifteen feet high. The parallelograms, 1 to 8, Pl. VIII. represent the total contents of such roofs; and the part covered with dark lines the proportion of each, which is opaque from the profile or breadth of the astragals, rafters, &c. while that covered by dotted lines represents the additional space rendered obscure by the shadows of these parts on the glass; taking the medium of each day's shadow. The section opposite each parallelogram represents the style of sash and roof; the price in the first column of prices is that of the sashes glazed and completed per foot; in the second the combined expense of the sashes, rafters, and supports, per foot; and the third column, the price per foot at which the part entirely transparent stands the purchaser.

Taking these parallelograms in another point of view, we may imagine each of them to represent a peach, grown in the sort of house the roof of which the figure represents. The black part of each parallelogram, or peach, may be supposed to represent insipidity or tartness, and the white part *aroma* or flavour. This will give a sensible notion of the difference in quality of the fruit produced by the different houses.—The parallelogram

No. 1. represents the contents of the glass roof of a house of the dimensions above detailed, and which is formed of solid iron astragals, tinned and placed eight inches apart, curved to the circumference of a circle whose radius is the width of the house, and with about one third part of the upper part of each astragal straight, as in *Fig. 3*, Pl. V. In the longitudinal part of this house there will be sixty astragals, each eighteen feet six inches long and five eighths of an inch wide, supported by two horizontal bars half an inch wide, and which bars extend the whole lengt of the house. The space darkened by these astragals and cross bars does not amount to five superficial feet. As the total contents of the space to be lighted (i. e. of a plane of a breadth equal to the hypothenuse of a right-angled triangle, whose base and sides are as the width and height, and whose length is that of the house) is 680 feet, this gives of opaque space 1-136th part of the whole. Add one fifth to the opaque space for the shadows of the astragals, and the total proportion does not amount to 1-114th part of the entire contents. In regard to light, therefore, this may be considered as perfect a roof as is practicable consistently with having the panes of glass of a moderate size. On comparing the columns of expense, repairs and durability, it will also be found the most œconomical in every other respect.

No. 2. The same as No. 1; but glazed in the ridge and furrow manner.

No. 3. Iron rafters every six feet, and light iron frames placed on them, to be raised by levers as in *Fig. 4*, Pl. V.

No. 4. Sashes four feet four inches broad, iron styles one inch and a quarter, and iron astragals, the styles of the one sash placed over those of the other, and screwed together, so that when finished the glass will be in two planes. The front sashes open, but the roof is fixed. This is an excellent plan for narrow houses, and in œconomy and durability comes nearest to No. 1. I have erected here a greenhouse, thirty feet long by ten feet broad, nearly on this plan.

No. 5. The same general plan as No. 4, but the astragals formed of wood.

No. 6. Wrought iron rafters, uprights, imposts, &c. the front sashes to open, and a part of the upper sashes to slide down; the whole nearly as in a specimen lately erected, in copper and iron, at the Union Nursery, King's Road, by Mr. Jorden of Birmingham.

No. 7. Cast iron standards, rafters, and imposts; the sashes with wooden frames, with an inner frame of iron, and filled in with wrought iron astragals. The rafters one inch and half broad, styles and rails two inches. Astragals three fourths of an inch. There are twelve rafters and twenty-four sloping sashes, which slide past each other, and eleven front sashes, which open outwards. This may be reckoned the most improved method at present in use for erecting common houses, and is the style I some time ago adopted in an extensive range at Dan y parc already mentioned.

No. 8. Constructed entirely of timber;—wooden uprights, imposts, rafters, styles, and rails. Rafters three inches broad and fourteen inches deep. The styles and rails two and half to three inches broad. The front lights sliding past each other. The whole according to the most recently erected wooden houses, as at Kensington Gardens, Kew Woodlands, Chiswick, Wanstead House, and even the curved wooden house erected by Mr. Palmer at Kingston.

On examining the table, it will be found that this style is by far the most expensive in respect to painting, and other annual repairs; and that its comparative durability is the least of the whole.

I am aware that tables of this description are liable to many objections, being generally exaggerated, so as to show the advantages of some one plan in preference to all others. I may however appeal to every experienced person in behalf of the moderation of that here presented. The first style, No. 1, admits of no dispute, as any reader may calculate the space darkened; and in respect to No. 8, or the wooden roofs, I am sure that every one will allow that if I had stated one half as the proportion rendered opaque by the massive rafters and clumsy sashes, it would not have been too much. Had I calculated the ends of all these houses, in connection with the roof, the proportion would have been much greater in favour of No. I. and against No. 8; for no form or plan is so well calculated to admit light as the quarter dome ends.

In most of the designs given in Pl. V. as well as for the hemispherical and campanulated house, I have recommended an outer curtain or canvass roofing. In respect to the benefits to be derived from adopting either an outer or inner curtain, I have never had any doubts; and so far back as 1804 I made several attempts by constructing models, and fitting up a house for public inspection at Edinburgh, at my own expense, as well as by publishing on the subject, to introduce them. From various causes, however, but chiefly from the force of prejudice, which in Scotland is particularly strong, they have been but very partially adopted. One reason, in as far as respects England, has been the want of conviction in the minds of gardeners that so slight a covering as a piece of thin canvass would have much effect;

but since Dr. Wells has published his valuable experiments on dew, the inutility of such a covering can no longer be pleaded as an excuse. The grand defects in this branch of horticultural œconomy have proceeded in general from inattention to the important fact illustrated by Professor Leslie, Count Rumford, Dr. Hoffman, and various others, " that radiating heat is subject in all cases to the optical laws which govern the reflection and refraction of light[1]." Hence the importance of placing a screen at a small distance from a heated body to reflect back the rays of heat which proceed from it in straight lines. The effect of such a screen, formed of a ragged cambric handkerchief, one yard square, placed horizontally over the surface of a grass plot, and so as to be six inches above it, but open on all sides, was to preserve a temperature from eight to eleven degrees higher than that of the grass fully exposed to the sky: " a difference," the doctor observes, " sufficiently great to explain the utility of a very slight shelter to plants, in averting or lessening injury from cold, on a still and severe night[2].

From all that I have been able to observe, much greater injury is sustained by plants from being overheated in the night-time, or from accidents happening to flues at that season, than by cold alone. To retain, by a double roofing, either of glass, canvass, boards, or otherwise, the heat obtained during the day, appears therefore a much safer mode than to trust to powerful fires, to be kept burning during the night, to supply the heat constantly radiating from the glass at that season, and lost in the atmosphere. Even in point of œconomy the double roofings deserve to be adopted in many situations, since they would both save fuel and nightly attendance. They are very generally used on the continent, and especially in the northern parts of Germany and Russia, where double windows are often adopted for the same purpose.

---

[1] Young's *Nat. Phil.* lect. li. p. 673.

[2] An *Essay on Dew, and several Appearances connected with it*: by W. C. Wells, M. D. F.R.S. London, 1814.

Independently of the safety and œconomy of these outer roofings, there is another advantage attending their use, which is by no means inconsiderable: this is, their preventing the inner surface of the glass from being covered with moisture or condensed exhalations, (as some gardeners call that appearance,) and which, by dropping all over the house, is so prejudicial to the plants. Some imagine that these dew-drops are formed chiefly from putrid effluvia exhaled from the plants, and that the only method of preventing them is to allow the foul air to escape or condense, by some contrivance in the upper part of the roof[1]. But the truth is, such drops are formed in an empty house in equal quantities as in one full of plants, under certain circumstances, viz. the cooling of the air of the house after having been heated to a degree considerably above that of the atmosphere.

With respect to the detail of construction of a canvass outer roofing, for the campanulated and globular houses, it should be formed in gores, so arranged as to wind up on rollers, which may be concealed under the projecting coping of the front or basement wall; and stout wires or iron rods bent to the same curve as the astragals of the roof are to be fixed, one end in the stone coping, and the other in the apex of the cone; and supported from the astragals at intervals, so as not to be less than ten inches from the glass. Then, by having slight rods or wires, like those used for fastening stair-carpets, attached across the gores, at the distance of every three or four feet, when drawn up by a cord and pulleys these cross rods would bear upon the long rods or ribs, and the rotundity of the roof would keep them so tight as to prevent their being disturbed by the wind.

If doubts are entertained on this head, the following contrivance may be adopted. Let each gore have a cord twice its length fixed at its narrow end, so that when the whole are drawn up in the evening, there will be as many long cords hanging down from the summit of the roof as there are gores. Half the cords, taking them alternately,

---

[1] Appendix to Abercrombie's *Practical Gardener*, 2d edition, 1817.

are then to be laid athwart the gores, and firmly tied to a hook, or to one of the rollers under the coping. The other half are also to be laid athwart and tied, but in a contrary direction, and so as to form the roof into lozenges, in the manner corn ricks are thatched in some districts. This plan would effectually prevent the gores from being ruffled by any wind whatever.

Where the roof is moveable, in the manner represented in the section Pl. VII. Fig. 3, of course no wire or rod for the gores to rest on is necessary, the line for opening the sashes answering every purpose.

In longitudinal houses, such as those in Pl. V. nothing can be more simple than their construction; and in all cases their expense is so moderate as to be no object. The trouble of working them twice a day will be reckoned an objection; but if they preserve from ten to fifteen degrees of heat, which would otherwise escape from the house and have to be made up by a larger supply of fuel, this will amply compensate for a little additional trouble.

As most of the foregoing improvements depend on the adoption of iron or other metals instead of wood, and as some eminent gardeners [1] do not consider that there have yet been sufficient trials of the former materials to justify the rejection of the latter, I shall here notice the objections commonly urged against metallic sashes and rafters. These objections have in almost every case proceeded either from the badness of the workmanship, a mere dislike to innovation, or from the use of improper metals; and they may be resolved into—

1. Breakage of glass, from the contraction and expansion of metallic sashes.
2. The conducting powers of metals, by which they carry off the heat.
3. Their liability to rust.
4. Their attraction of the electricity.

---

[1] Abercrombie, and Mean in Abercrombie's *Practical Gardener*, App.—also Nicol in *Villa Garden Directory*, &c.

1. The effects of change of temperature are acknowledged to be inconvenient where a frame, entirely constructed of metal, is tightly fitted into grooves, in which it is intended to slide; or even in rabbets to be opened by hinges. It is acknowledged also, that copper or brass frames are more liable to this objection than such as are formed of iron; the expansibility of these metals being as 95 and 89 to 60. But frames formed wholly of metal, and fitted into grooves, in which they are expected to slide, or move readily by hinges, form no part of the designs which have been submitted, nor will, I am persuaded, form a part of any good plan. The iron roofs which I have recommended are either wholly fixed, or the moveable sashes are laid on the rafters, and the styles of the one sash placed over those of the other alternately; or, they are iron frames fitted into wooden frames; in either of which cases their contraction and expansion will not affect their motion, nor occasion their twisting.

The breakage of glass has resulted chiefly from the twisting of long astragals, composed of broad narrow hoops of copper or brass, soldered or otherwise attached to a narrow moulding of the same metals or of lead, and not sufficiently strengthened by cross bars. This defect is to be remedied by making the rabbet and moulding stronger, and by lessening the distance between the bearing bars. In solid iron astragals, however, it cannot take place.

It can seldom happen that the mere expansion of iron in length can be the cause of the breakage of glass. Dr. Young[1] states the expansion of that metal to be $\frac{1}{\ldots}$ of its length for each degree of eleva-

---

[1] Lect. li. Sir George Mackenzie, in the 2d vol. of the *Edin. Hort. Trans.* mentions the expansion of glass as occasioning its breakage; but as the expansibility of this material is still less than that of iron (Young), and as the panes are seldom more than eight inches square, and are bedded in putty, it is difficult to conceive any degree of expansion produced from our atmosphere capable of producing any practical effect. If according to Dalton the expansion of thin glass be nearly as that of iron, then astragals of that metal will be less likely to occasion breakage than wooden sashes.

tion of temperature: hence, supposing an elevation of fifty degrees, an astragal or rod of twenty feet in length would only be increased one inch and one third, or less than one line per foot, which could have no sensible effect.

As I propose in almost every case to use curved rafters, and astragals instead of front and sloping glass, that circumstance will have a tendency to direct what expansion there may take place outwards, and thus to prevent twisting.

In respect to copper, glass has certainly been broken in several cases from the too great length of astragals formed of that metal, which expands with every degree of heat $\frac{1}{100000}$ part; and hence the expansion in an astragal of twenty feet would be nearly two inches; which might do injury: but independently of this objection, the deleterious nature of the rust of this metal ought to exclude it from every description of hothouse.

2. The objections drawn from the conducting powers of metals, in respect to heat, are of a more serious nature; but though they cannot be entirely removed, they admit, in common with every other evil, of being greatly alleviated, if not of being rendered practically of no force. In greenhouses and such glass cases as do not require a high temperature during the winter months, this capacity of metals is of little consequence; but in stoves, in early forcing-houses, and in hotbed frames, its influence will be severely felt if not counteracted. The means of counteraction are *painting*, which lessens in a considerable degree the conducting as it increases the radiating powers of metals; where iron rafters are used, covering their inner edges with a *slip of wood*; and tinning[1] iron astragals lessens in a slight degree the conducting power of that metal, and prevents its rusting. But the most complete mode is by applying an outer curtain, as before described. This remedy is simple, œconomical, and effectual. Where these pre-

---

[1] The conducting powers of the metals are as under, viz. gold, silver, copper, iron, tin, lead.

cautions are neglected or imperfectly adopted, the lost heat must be made good by increasing the supply from the flues: but I may repeat, as an important consideration, that it is always safer to preserve the heat already in the house, than to let it escape, and depend on the generation of more from the flues. I would therefore for known reasons strongly recommend the adoption of an outer or inner roofing in every description of stove or early forcing-house [1].

M. A. Thouin [2], the botanical professor to the Museum of Natural History at Paris, has, in as far as respects their conducting capacities, urged the objections to iron frames with more force and ingenuity than any English writer. He had adopted in the *Jardin des Semis* frames entirely of iron for some hotbeds and pits constructed there for raising tender seeds. He found the iron expand in summer, so as to become too light for the grooves, and in winter their conducting powers carried off great part of the heat. As the frames are of very clumsy manufacture, and the mass of iron large in proportion to the volume of heated air within; and as in some of the pits there is no flue to supply the heat as it is withdrawn, and no outer curtain to retain it in any of them, the effect must undoubtedly be considerable. The remedy is only to be found in a complete outer curtain, or in a better original construction. The astragals alone should have been of iron; not the styles and rails; and by having them attached to an inner frame, such as will be afterwards described, the effects of contraction and expansion would not have been felt as an injury, and all the advantages of iron frames (which M. Thouin allows to be great) retained. It is obvious that the larger the volume of heated air, the

---

[1] In the *Niederlandische Hesperides*, by Commelines, an old Dutch book on the culture of oranges and their preservation during winter in cellars, greenhouses, &c. the author mentions an amateur who bestowed great attention and expense on their culture, but whose trees never looked so well as those of a less opulent neighbour. On inquiry, he found his gardener used as many baskets of turf in one year, as his poor friend did in three. The obvious conclusion which Commelines draws from this circumstance is not without application in our own times.

[2] *Essai sur l'Exposition et la Division méthodique de l'Œconomie rurale*, &c. Paris, 1814.

longer time it will require to cool; and consequently the conducting power of an iron roof will be injurious inversely as the size of the house. As the conducting power would from the greater cold of the atmosphere be greatest in the night-time, it may be considered that an outer curtain would counteract it sufficiently for all practical purposes; and it appears to me, no person who *consulted taste* (even while he might *study utility*) would ever put the expense of an outer curtain, or some additional loads of fuel, in competition with the great advantages of metallic houses in point of *admission of light, durability, elegance, and susceptibility of any shape and magnitude.*

3. The objections taken from the rusting of metallic substances, and especially of iron and copper, if one may judge from some houses recently erected of the latter material, are not without force. In respect to iron, the cause of rust is to be found in bad workmanship; and is to be remedied by the important precaution of first fitting all the iron work together at the foundry or manufactory, and then taking it to pieces, heating it nearly to a red heat, and applying a coat of coal tar or common paint. Engineers[1] have found that iron so heated will not rust for many years. Heating copper and brass previously to painting these metals, has little or no effect on them; but even if it had the deleterious nature of the rust of these metals—the risk of their exhibiting some rusty spots even under the best treatment—the certainty that they must in the end, in common with all metals, decay through oxidation—these things, coupled with the circumstances of some families having been nearly poisoned by the verdigrise dropping from copper astragals on grapes and cucumbers, ought to prevent the use of that metal in hothouses in any form, or under any disguise whatever.

Tin and lead, but especially pewter, do not rust, or their oxidation is so slow, as that, speaking practically, it amounts to nothing. As, in addition to this, they are worse conductors of heat than iron, their use as

---

[1] Fulton in *Treatise on Canals.*

mouldings to iron rabbets, or for coating over solid iron astragals, is of considerable importance.

4. The conducting powers of metals in respect to electricity have been urged against their adoption in hothouses; but this objection hardly requires answering. Where they are entirely of iron they may be considered as one large conductor; where partially, a proper conductor may be applied. If this objection were tenable, what would have become of iron foundries? Besides, there are houses entirely of iron which have been in existence from five to fifteen years, without sustaining or occasioning any injury[1].

These are the ostensible objections; but the real cause why metallic houses are so seldom erected has but little connexion with them. From the comparative difficulties of their execution, the regular hothouse builders do not like to meddle with them; and it is not likely, speaking generally, that either architects, builders, or tradesmen in *full employ* will take the trouble, and go to the expense of introducing an article, or perfecting a construction, from which they could gain nothing more than what they already possess—namely, a sufficient business. If the professional aid of a regular architect or hothouse builder is not called in by the party about to erect a house, the design and execution are left to the gardener, who generally is obliged to have recourse to the carpenter of his employer, and of course wood is his material. These circumstances would materially increase the expense of metallic houses to such private gentlemen as thought of attempting their adoption; and to the same cause has conspired the use of the more expensive metals, such as copper, brass, tin, or other compounds, instead of the cheaper and more durable article, iron. As œconomy is always an object pursued by every one, the first cost has also retarded their introduction, though this fancied œconomy will, in this instance at least, be found to end in its opposite[2].

---

[1] Mr. Blackburne's vinery near Preston, a conservatory at Windsor, at East Sheen, &c.
[2] See the table in Pt. VIII.

PART II.

On the Detail of Construction, and on Execution.

THE noblest design, badly executed, is disagreeable to the view, and ruinous to the proprietor of the edifice. Bad foundations and roofs, improper materials, materials of different degrees of durability piled incongruously together, and bad workmanship, form the elements of bad execution. In no country are materials and labour obtained in greater perfection than in England; and in all regular works, coming under the architect or engineer, we generally find little to condemn, and much to admire in the execution of the work[1]. Hothouses, how-

---

[1] Take the grand lock at the western junction of the Caledonian Canal with the ocean, by Mr. Telford, and the Strand Bridge by Mr. Rennie, as examples in Britain, and the cones of Cherburg, and the *Pont des Arts*, in France. In general, however, execution on the continent is far inferior, though the designs in respect to an accurate adjustment of the means to the end in the engineering art, and of classic taste in architecture, are often superior, to those of British artists. In Russia and Poland the noblest buildings are frequently rendered contemptible by the clumsiness of the labour, and the discordancy of the materials. In one of the finest efforts of the celebrated Imperial architect the Chevalier de Quaringhi, l'Hopital de Chérémétow, in Moscow, which is built of brick and stuccoed, and is on the whole one of the best executed edifices in the empire, the finishing balustrade is of timber, each baluster a thin board, coloured and shaded to imitate stone. To commemorate the spot at Kiow where Vladimir embraced the Christian religion, and threw his idols into the Dnieper, the present Emperor erected a magnificent column in 1802. The situation both by nature and association of ideas is grand; and in design the monument corresponds; but executed in brick and timber plastered and painted, it fails to communicate the leading idea of a monument, *durability;* and in fact in 1814 was literally tumbling to pieces. Hothouses in these countries are sometimes grand in design, but always ephemeral in duration.

ever, and garden buildings in general, are in some degree an anomalous class, and more the subject of chance or caprice in design, and of local convenience in execution, than those of any department of rural architecture.

The subject till very lately has not been deemed of sufficient importance to render it worth an architect's time to make himself master of the first step towards improvement in every art, the knowledge of what has already been done by others; and on this account the amount of some recent attempts has not exceeded local variation of form. Scientific gardeners are certainly the best judges, and ought to be the best designers of hothouses; though their other avocations, and their localization, too often prevent them from attending to the whole subject scientifically. Each may develop new practices within his own sphere of action; but it requires time, and much general observation, to embody so many scattered hints in a general system of improved construction. Hence that variety of plans which are observable in different gardens, and the number of patents and published designs which have from time to time attracted public attention. It is true, as Mr. Knight observes, that this variety is a proof of the infancy of art; but still it evinces at the same time a strong tendency to perfection.

The leading features of all the modern improvements will be noticed in the following remarks, in which I shall chiefly study brevity, convinced from experience that more may be done in a subject of this nature by manufacturing establishments, in which improvements may be at once embodied, and exposed for public sale; than by any didactic work, however perfect or minute. An arrangement of this description will shortly be put in activity in London, in which every improvement hinted at in this work, and all future improvements as they may come into notice, will constantly be attended to; and when of due value rendered available to the public as articles of trade.

The remarks submitted, are in the order following; viz. SITUATION, DESIGN, MODE OF HEATING, MODE OF VENTILATING, and EXECUTION.

(49)

The obvious and customary SITUATION for culinary hothouses is in the kitchen garden; for greenhouses or conservatories, in the parterre or shrubbery, or attached to the mansion. But modern taste has in some instances judiciously disposed the whole in one magnificent range *en suite* with the principal apartments of the house, and this is perhaps one of the greatest luxuries of a modern country residence. When subsequent improvements in communicating heat, and in ventilation, shall have rendered the artificial climates produced, equal or superior to those which they imitate, then will such an appendage to a family seat be not less useful in a medical point of view, than elegant and luxurious as a lounge for exercise or entertainment in inclement weather. Perhaps the time may arrive when such artificial climates will not only be stocked with appropriate birds, fishes, and harmless animals, but with examples of the human species from the different countries imitated, habited in their particular costumes, and who may serve as gardeners or curators of the different productions. But this subject is too new and strange to admit of discussion, without incurring the ridicule of general readers.

The most extensive range of glass houses attached to a mansion which I have any where seen (and as glass houses are almost entirely confined to Britain and the north of Europe, I may say I have seen every hothouse of any consequence in the world,) is at Gorinka, the magnificent domain of Count Razumówski, near Moscow. The house is in the centre, and the glass forms two wings fronting the lawn, the whole composing an immense semicircle terminating in one extremity in a building dedicated to natural history, and containing an extensive collection under the superintendance of an eminent professor (Fischer). The other ending in a theatre, capable like that at Versailles of being arranged as a ball-room, concert-room, tennis-court, or riding-house, in a few hours[1].

---

[1] Independently of this range, there are at Gorinka nearly thirty detached houses in the botanic garden, there being in all above three English acres covered with glass. For how much

In England there are several magnificent orangeries attached to mansions, but few instances of all the glass being in one range and *en suite*. In general, where there is the greatest number of houses, as in the Royal gardens, Woodlands, St. Fagons, &c. they are scattered and disconnected in such a way as to produce no effect. To be under the necessity of walking some distance from the mansion before you enter the conservatory, and then to be exposed to the open air between the inspection of each of the remaining glass houses, appears to me *mal-adroit* and insalutary.

The DESIGN or plan to be adopted depends on the combined considerations arising from the situation and the object in view. Where a range, or a single house, is to be attached to a mansion, study elegance; but where the kitchen garden is selected as the place of erection, study utility and œconomy. As in the present mode of construction in timber, perpendicular front glass of two or three feet in height, and a sloping roof placed to an angle of forty or forty-five degrees, have been long found to answer most purposes, at least for vines, greenhouses, and botanic stoves; so, as a general design for corresponding objects, and adapted for iron astragals, I propose that of which *Figs.* 1, 2, and 3, PL. V. are delineations. For peach-houses for a general crop, the same form may be adopted, with the glass in three or more parts, to be raised as in *Fig.* 4, PL. V. For fruiting pineries, I have no hesitation in saying that the section in PL. V. *Fig.* 7, though inconvenient as to keeping the plants perpendicular in the bark pit, yet is in principle far superior to any in common use, and, if steam were substituted for bark, would in theory be as perfect in respect to the slope of the glass and pit as the nature of the subject admits. The earliest

---

mankind depend on this elegant material produced from seemingly the most useless of the *débris* of our globe, see a most eloquent paper by Professor Cuvier, in the *Magasin Encyclopédique* for 1816, entitled *Réflexions sur la Marche actuelle des Sciences, et sur leurs Rapports avec la Société*. See also *A didactic Epistle to General Showalow on the Utility of Glass*: Petersburg 1760, by the celebrated Russian poet and philosopher Lomonosow.

description of forcing-houses, whether for grapes or peaches, will be most advantageously arranged after the manner of *Fig.* 6, Pl. 1, with the improvements and variations of which that plan is susceptible.

As leading general data on this subject I submit the following, viz.

1. That where the glass is to be fixed[1], the roof should be formed of astragals alone. See Pl. V. *Figs.* 1, 2, and 3, and the explanation to these figures.
2. That in almost every case curved cast iron rafters, proceeding at once from the front to the back wall, will be preferable to having upright front glass, as affording much more light, admitting the improved method of giving air shown in Pl. VII., as well as being more elegant and less expensive. See *Fig.* 4, Plate V.
3. An outer or inner curtain will be found of great service in every case; and it has this peculiar property, that, if it does no good, it cannot possibly do harm.
4. Wherever a number of houses are together, and placed under the management of a careful person, they will be best heated by steam.
5. In addition to every house, there ought to be in the back shed or other adjoining building a reservoir of temperate air.
6. In addition to the best arrangements and the most expert gardener, the artificial regulator of temperature invented by Mr. Kewley will be found of real utility.
7. In remote parts of the country, on a small scale, and under

---

[1] Air admitted from the front wall and back wall, it would appear, is found sufficient in the case of vines; at least judging from Mr. Knight's experience, which, as a German critic judiciously observes, is particularly important, and has occasioned considerable improvement in England in this branch. "*Die erfahrungen des Herrn Knight ueber diesen gegenstand sind besonders wichtig, und wir empfehlen sie vorzüglich dem Deutschen leser, da sie in diesem anlegen weit fortschritte in England gemacht hat.*" Göttingische Gelehrte Anzeigen, Jan. 1817, p. 146.

ordinary circumstances, simple improvements, and such as when they go out of order can be readily repaired by local artists, should be adopted in preference to more perfect plans which require greater skill in the management, and more expert artisans to reinstate them in case of derangement.

HEAT is artificially communicated to hothouses by fire, steam, and the putrefactive fermentation of vegetable substances. Heating by fires is the most ancient and general mode. Originally in this country hot embers were placed in a hole in the floor[1]. On the continent, fires were made in stoves erected within the house[2]; and subsequently they were kindled at one end of a large vault under the floor, the smoke going out by a chimney at the other[3]. To these plans succeeded horizontal flues[4], reserve chambers of heated air[5], air flues[6], and the introduction of hot air through metallic tubes in contact with the fire[7]. One Watts, gardener to the company of Apothecaries at Chelsea, in 1684, seems to have been the first to convey heat by tunnels underneath the floor of his greenhouse[8]; and Evelyn[7], a few years after, gives a plan for introducing a constant supply of heated air from the fire-place, very similar to the mode for which a patent has been recently obtained by the Marquis de Chabannes[9]. The various alterations and

---

[1] Ray's *Letters*, 172. This was originally the practice in private houses, and hence the curfew or *couvre feu*, &c. See Beckmann's *History of Inventions*, vol. ii. p. 103.

[2] Parkinson's *Herbal*, p. 588. *Niederlandische Hesperides*, 145.

[3] *Ecole du Potager*, Paris, 1750; and Kirchner's *Praktische Anleitung für Gartenkunst*, &c. Leipsig, 1796.

[4] Linnæus in *Descriptio Horti Upsaliensis*. *Maison rustique*, 3ieme edit. art. Serre.

[5] *Encyclopédie Méthodique*, art. Serre. Van Oosten in *Dutch Gardener*, 1711.

[6] Dr. Anderson in *Patent Hothouse*, and in *Recreations*.

[7] Evelyn in *Kalendarium Hortense*, App. to 4th edit. Gouger in *Méchanique du Feu*, Paris, 1713, and *La Maison rustique*, p. 14, tom. ii. edit. 1768.

[8] Martyn in Miller's *Dictionary*, art. Stove.

[9] *Explanation of a new Method for warming and purifying the Air in private Houses*, &c. London, 1815. Gouger's work, translated and improved by Desaguliers in 1715, contains the rudiments of the Marquis de Chabannes, and almost every other modern improvement in toves and fire places.

(53)

improvements that have been made from Evelyn's time to the present day, are so numerous as not to admit even of recapitulation in these Remarks. Most of them may be found in the Repertory of Arts, and the principal French and English Encyclopedias, particularly that of Dr. Rees. In as far as respects hothouses, the subject has been treated of in the most ingenious manner by Dr. Anderson; and Mons. Guyton in the *Annales de Chimie* has given the ablest view of its œconomy for domestic and general purposes.

The earliest proposal which I have met with for forwarding vegetation by steam is contained in the Gentleman's Magazine for January 1755; and the first who actually practised steam forcing appears to have been Mr. Wakefield of Liverpool in 1788. Mr. Hoyle of Halifax took out a patent for heating hothouses and other buildings by steam in 1791. Mr. Butler employed steam with success in a pinery at Knowlsby in Lancashire in 1792, and Mr. Green in dwelling-houses and greenhouses in London in 1793[1]. Mr. Mawer of Dalry near Edinburgh adopted steam in 1794[2] in three pineries, two peachhouses, and two vineries, and Mr. Weston of Leicester, in pits about the same time. Subsequently Mr. Thomson, at Tynningham[3], Mr. Williams[4], Dr. Lisle[5], Mr. Dennison[6], and various others, down to Mr. Fraser[7], who at the Royal gardens at Kensington has recently commenced his operations for heating by steam more scientifically than (as far as I know) has hitherto been done. In all the above instances, excepting Hoyle's and Fraser's, the steam was admitted to mix with the air of the house, and condense on the plants;

---

[1] *Repertory of Arts.* Buchannan on *Heating by Steam*, p. 164.
[2] Robertson's *View of the Agriculture of Mid Lothian*, Appendix, Edinburgh, 1798.
[3] The Earl of Haddington's seat near Dunbar.
[4] London *Hort. Trans.* vol. i.
[5] At St. Fagons near Cardiff.
[6] At Dorking: steam is also employed in a hothouse at Clapham, and at Mr. Loddige's nursery, Hackney.
[7] Ironmonger and Brazier, Long Acre, London.

a mode which effectually destroys insects, and may therefore be occasionally resorted to; but which, considered merely as supplying artificial heat, is attended with the greatest uncertainty. The only work which has yet appeared on the subject of heating generally by steam, is that of the late able engineer Mr. Buchannan [1].

Probably the most ancient mode of forcing is that by the use of fermenting vegetable substances. It is mentioned by Lord Bacon as a thing common in his time [2], and in *L'Ecole Potagere* by Combles, *La Maison rustique*, Quinteney, Bénard, and other old French authors on gardening and rural affairs, as long practised in their country for raising cucumbers and melons. Laurence is the first English author who proposes using dung to force his favourite fruit the grape; and from the time of this writer to the present day, it has been occasionally adopted on a limited scale for this and similar purposes, though from the limited supply it is not likely to come into general use, otherwise than for hotbeds or pits. Speechley and M‘Phail have best treated the subject of moist heat, as it is called, and the construction of dungpits and hotbeds.

Other modes of heating may be occasionally resorted to, such as from the waste hot water of a distillery or brewery, hot ashes from a foundry, hot springs, &c. as at Matlock and Tœplitz, where hothouses might be thus heated; but their occurrence is too rare to merit consideration here.

Of the two first modes of communicating artificial heat, that by STEAM has been found much the best for warming the air of manufactories and dwelling-houses, from its greater regularity, from its susceptibility of being conveyed to any distance at an uniform temperature, and from the greater salubrity of the heat produced [3]. That

---

[1] *A Treatise on the Œconomy of Fuel, and on Heating and Drying by means of Steam*, by Robertson Buchannan, Civil Engineer. Glasgow, 1815.

[2] *Philosophical Works*, by Shaw, articles Vegetation and Tobacco.

[3] See Buchannan's work above referred to: also Rees's *Cyclopædia*, art. Steam.

its introduction into hothouses would be attended with equally beneficial effects, a slight general comparison between steam and fire heat will show.

1. Fire heat is communicated to a hothouse by an arrangement which gives the power of heating a certain quantity of masonry, or metallic tubes, to an unlimited degree. If the heat is to be increased, it is produced by an increase of the quantity of fuel. The heat from steam is communicated by a similar arrangement; but as that fluid under common circumstances cannot be rendered hotter than boiling water, the thermometer applied to any part of a steam pipe generally rising to 190°, an increase of heat is produced by an increase of the surface to be heated. As quantity or dimension is obviously much more readily subjected to calculation than the effects to be produced on a flue or stove by increased combustion, there must be greater certainty and less risk of extremes in heating by steam than by fire.

2. In the best arrangements of flues in a hothouse, or of grates and stoves in rooms or manufactories, it is extremely difficult to equalize the temperature in every part of the heated space; that end of the flue nearest the fire always remaining the hottest, and may exhibit 500° where it enters the house, while fifty feet distant or at the other end it does not show 50°; because air and smoke, the two mediums employed to convey the heat from the fires, are the very worst conductors of heat. In the use of steam, even with no great attention to the distribution of the tubes, a perfectly equal temperature is constantly produced; because the vapour of water is the best known carrier of heat, and a tube filled with steam is no hotter at one yard than it is at one hundred yards from the boiler; but in every part of its length will raise a thermometer applied within an inch of the tube to 190° or 200 degrees.

3. Fire heat conveyed in flues gives out dust and smoke, mixed with decomposed atmospheric air, in quantities depending on the materials and workmanship of the flue. Iron stoves when heated intensely are supposed to decompose the watery part of the atmo-

sphere, by which hydrogen gas is evolved, and an unwholesome and disagreeable smell produced. Steam is not liable to these bad effects: for the tubes of metal by which it is conveyed can be made so strong and tight as to prevent the escape of steam; and if even some were to escape, its effects in a hothouse would be favourable to vegetation, and in a house much less filthy and deleterious than smoke, dust, and hydrogen gas[1].

4. Flues "such as we use," as Sir Joseph Banks judiciously observes, "waste in the walls which conceal them more than half the warmth they receive from the fires which heat them;" but by a judiciously contrived furnace and steam boiler[2] very little heat will be lost. The œconomy of fuel therefore by steam must be very considerable. In a single pinery of ordinary dimensions, such as that at Kensington, it may be taken at more than three fourths of that used there; but where ten houses are to be heated from one boiler, the saving would probably be upwards of eight tenths. The saving in the first erection would be at least one half in an extensive range, though perhaps little or nothing in the case of a single house; and in all probability the saving in attendance and management would be as great as that of fuel.

If the advantages of heating by steam in hothouses are, or promise to be, so considerable, it may be asked why, having been tried for nearly twenty years, it has not become more general. To this I answer, that in respect to the trials mentioned above, they were exceedingly imperfect; and that the steam was applied more as dew or moisture, than as a vehicle for communicating heat. In the range of houses at Dalry, in which steam was so extensively used, fire heat was also employed in the usual manner and proportion; the boilers were

---

[1] Mr. Buchannan observes, that wherever steam had been adopted for heating the cotton mills, the persons employed, who used to be emaciated and sallow where stoves were used, had regained their health and assumed a fresh appearance. p. 207.

[2] Such as that mentioned by McNaught in Buchannan's work; or as greatly improved by Mr. Fraser at Kensington, and at Mr. Andrews's pineries, Vauxhall.

placed over the furnaces, and the steam was conducted along the paths of the houses in earthen pipes, and allowed at intervals to escape into the air of the house, and condense on the glass and plants. From this arrangement, which was expensive, no other advantages, as I have elsewhere stated [1], resulted (unless that the steam was more pure) than what are obtainable from pouring water on hot flues. Mr. Williams admits the steam to a vault, which is a very good method for supplying bottom heat; but a proper trial has not yet been made for heating the air of hothouses in the same manner employed at the cotton-mills and other manufactories in the neighbourhood of Glasgow. I have already mentioned the trials commenced at Kensington, and at the pineries of Mr. Andrews, by Mr. Fraser; and if he meets with that encouragement to which his knowledge of the subject, experience, and laudable desire of improvement seem eminently to entitle him, this elegant and healthful mode of supplying heat will soon become general not only in hothouses, but in all extensive concerns requiring an artificial temperature [2].

In respect to the objections to the use of steam in hothouses, I know of none that are not equally applicable to the introduction of steam in private houses or manufactories; and experience shows that these have been readily got over. The supposed trouble of nightly attendance in hothouses which Mr. Buchannan mentions, he also observes is rapidly giving way to improvements in the construction of the boilers and stoves. At Kensington no more attention is required in the nighttime than is requisite for a common furnace; and if one of Mr. Kewley's machines were adopted, there would only be the trouble of filling a large hopper with coals once in twenty-four hours, as Mr. K.'s apparatus would regulate the temperature of the house, and the boiler would regulate itself.

---

[1] *Short Treatise on Hothouses.*

[2] Mr. Buchannan in p. 293 observes, that "steam begins to come into use for heating hothouses," but does not refer to any examples. Since I began this part of these Remarks I have learned that Mr. Loddige, nurseryman at Hackney, is making arrangements to heat the whole of his extensive hothouses by steam.

I

Perhaps the difficulty of procuring and erecting the apparatus may deter some from adopting steam. But surely in Britain this must be an imaginary difficulty. In the most distant provinces it is only necessary to put Buchannan's work already mentioned into the hands of an experienced millwright, or to send him to examine some house or factory heated by steam. Near London every patriotic improver will of course employ Mr. Fraser, who has the greatest merit, and deserves every encouragement for having tried the scheme in the Royal Gardens at his own expense and risk.

I shall only add, as a general idea, that in large establishments where the mansion, the family stables, the farm, and the garden, are all at some distance from each other[1], it will be worth while to have separate apparatus for each of these departments. But in smaller mansions and in villas, where the whole are grouped together[2], one boiler may serve the varied purposes of heating the hothouses, the mansion, and such appendages as baths, laundries, malt-kilns, cattle-steamers, poultry-houses, &c. It may also, if thought desirable, have arrangements which can be put in and out of work at pleasure, for impelling mill- and grind-stones, a thrashing-machine, turnip-cutters and washers, straw-cutters, a fire-engine in case of fire, and for effecting a variety of other purposes, one of which, very obviously useful, is that of forcing water to an elevated reservoir, so as to supply water-closets, water-cocks, &c. in different parts of the house or hothouses, and *jets-d'eau* in the gardens. The principal apartments of the house and all the hothouses might be self-regulated by Mr. Kewley's machine; and for the general care of the engine, thrashing- and other machines, it will always be advisable to have a millwright[3] on

---

[1] As at Woburn Abbey, Alnwick Castle, Harewood House, &c.

[2] As at Garth House near Welch Pool, where an extensive range of hothouses (the only part of the design in which my plans were not followed) unite the mansion with the farm-yard and a range of circular stables, the latter perhaps the most elegant in England.

[3] As most of the improvements in rural œconomy, and indeed in every branch of human art, depend much on the perfection and constant good order of machinery, I would suggest to country gentlemen the advantages to be derived from having a good millwright on their estates.

the spot with a labourer at his command. In this case a gasometer might advantageously be added, and the premises both internally and externally, as far as necessary for general use and occasional splendour, lighted with gas. The cost of a complete gasometer capable of supporting forty lights for four hours, and each light equal to ten candles of eight in the pound, is said to be 250 pounds [1]. Six pounds of coal produce light equal to one pound of tallow, and there remains the value of the coke. The cost of the steam apparatus depends much on the distance which the parts to be heated are from one another; but the additional comfort, and saving in the attendance and insurance, will generally far counterbalance the expense of the first erection.

As it is not likely that steam will soon, if ever, become so general as to supersede in horticultural buildings the use of smoke flues, a few remarks are submitted on the improvements which have been recently attempted in the œconomy of fire heat in hothouses.

In order to obtain the greatest effects from a given quantity of fuel, Dr. Anderson in his patent hothouse (February 1801) proposes a large smoke chamber under or adjoining the house, so far not unlike the old Dutch practice already mentioned, but with the addition of an air chamber over or around it, and communicating by valves with the house. The plan is simple, and may occasionally be adopted with advantage. In various places [2] attempts have been made to col-

---

The nature of the employment of this superior class of mechanics leads them to think and judge accurately respecting mechanical operations in general;—there are few of the common machines of country carpenters and smiths that they will not improve on, and they are always ready to invent some expedient in a case of extremity. I consider myself fortunate in having at present a millwright, Mr. William Ward, as my foreman, very competent to heating by steam, lighting by gas, or to execute any improvement suggested in these Remarks.

[1] Clegg in *Philosophical Journal*, vol. xxiii. p. 86. Mr. Rucker's mansion near London, Mr. Lee's at Manchester, and Pitkellony House in Fifeshire, are heated by steam. Mr. Lee's house, and Lord Gray's in Perthshire, are lighted by gas.

[2] At Abercairnie near Crief, Perthshire, in 1790; at Manchester about 1770.

lect part of the heat, which is otherwise lost or absorbed in the mass of brickwork containing the furnaces outside the house. The fuel-chamber is surrounded by a vacuity, either communicating directly with the house a few feet from the furnace, or with an air flue or tube which conveys the heat thus collected, to the middle or opposite end of the house. Sometimes also heated air is generated by cast iron plates[1] or tubes placed over or on each side the fire or furnace, on the same general principle recommended by Evelyn, Gouger[2], and Chabannes; but as I have formerly observed, the warmth produced from very hot iron never being so wholesome as that produced from stone or earthen-ware, this variety merits adoption in but few cases. In general it may be observed, that the hot air introduced by air flues is so much deprived of its moisture when the fire is brisk, and so liable to vary in its temperature in the night-time, that it becomes unadvisable to use it exclusively as a mode of supplying heat; but in connexion with common smoke flues, the air flue conducted upon or around them, tends to equalize the heat given out to the house, which without this improvement is commonly much too great near the furnace. In foggy weather, and when the air is in a certain state in respect to exhalations and moisture, by opening the valves of the air flue, and admitting a stream of this exsiccated air, it may tend, Mr. Stuart[3] observes, to prevent "damps and mildews." Wherever the introduction of heated air forms a material part of a plan, a hygrometer should be used to regulate the degree of moisture in the house; and care should be taken that the fuel chamber is in a state of perfect repair, otherwise smoke will sometimes find its way through crevices in the brick-

---

[1] At Archerfield in East Lothian, and various other houses near Edinburgh; and ingeniously varied at Mr. Henderson's nursery gardens at Brechin.

[2] See in his *Méchanique du Feu*, Paris 1713, a description of a chimney with the back, hearth, and jambs of hollow iron, to heat the air that is to enter the room;—also his plan of conducting the air so heated to different rooms, &c.

[3] Specification of his Patent for heating and ventilating Hothouses and other Buildings, March 1801.

work into the air chamber, where mingling with the heated air, it will be conveyed to the house, than which there is nothing more injurious to vegetation [1].

With respect to improvements on smoke flues, none of importance have been recently made, that are not nearly coeval with their original introduction.

Mr. Stuart and the late Mr. Kyle[2] observe, that the air ought to have free access to them on all sides, and that they ought to traverse the house lengthways as low and as near the front glass as possible. Mr. Stevenson[3] has recommended flues of larger dimensions than usual in this country, but which have been long in use among the Dutch[4]. Sir George Mackenzie recommends zig-zag or embrasure flues[5], which is in effect nearly the same with a plan I once tried of

---

[1] By attempting to collect the heated air generated between the outer and inner furnace doors, in 1804 and -5, the description of furnace which I then adopted in the experimental house at Edinburgh before mentioned, became liable to this objection, whenever by change of wind or otherwise the fire did not draw well. As some plants were injured by the smoke and too great heat introduced in the night-time, a fine opportunity was thereby given to Mr. Nicol and others of the old school, with whom

"No crime so great as daring to excell,"

to decry indiscriminately in subsequent publications the whole system of heated air, double roofings, and other improvements, without displaying the slightest knowledge of the principles on which these improvements were proposed; but *De mortuis nil, &c.* Double roofings some of the Scotch horticulturists affect to treat with ridicule, and this with Professor Leslie in their capital, than whom no man has so ably shown in theory the immense advantages derivable from their use. See his *Experiments on the concentric Cases*, pages 373-8. By concentric hand glasses I have no doubt of being able to preserve a pine plant during winter in the open garden without the aid of artificial heat.

[2] Gardener to Baron Stuart at Moredun, whom Dr. Duncan mentions as an eminent promoter of gardening in Scotland, and who "used nearly fifty years ago to boast of producing every fruit in perfection but apples and pears." Mr. Kyle is author of a *Treatise on Forcing Vines and Peaches*, Edinburgh 1778, now very scarce.

[3] Caledonian *Hort. Trans.* vol. i.

[4] See *Fig.* 6, Pl. I. also the section of the Dutch *serre chaude* in *Encyc. Méthod.* plates to vol. d'Aratoire, &c.

[5] Caledonian *Hort. Trans.* vol. ii.

compartment flues[1]; but both these modes of increasing the surface to be heated, are liable to the objections of retarding the progress of the smoke, and consequently of accumulating the heat too much at the end next the fire; besides rendering it impossible to clean them without adopting the abominable practice of introducing boys for that purpose. Mr. Lorimer[2] found can flues answer, which Dr. Duncan[3] is inclined to think a serious improvement. They have been long in use more or less both in Britain and on the continent[4]. As they are soon heated and soon cooled, they are not to be depended on for a regular temperature, especially in the night-time; but being œconomical, of easy carriage and readily put together, they deserve adoption in several cases, and especially under temporary glass roofs placed against hot walls. When used in permanent houses they should be wholly or partially immersed in coarse sand as in Holland, by which means their characteristic defects are in a considerable degree remedied. From forming a more perfect tube or funnel than a brick flue, it is probable the heat given out by can flues will be more salutary than that emitted from those constructed of the former material; from the numerous joints of which smoke and decomposed air sometimes escape to contaminate the atmosphere of the house. In connexion with an outer or inner curtain, which will prevent any house from cooling in one night to a pernicious degree, I should have no hesitation in adopting them generally, as being cheap, simple, easily transported and erected, and less liable to the objection of Sir Joseph Banks, that of "wasting in the walls which enclose them half the warmth they receive from the fires which heat them."

---

[1] *Short Treatise on Hothouses*, sect. li. p. 33.
[2] Caledonian *Hort. Trans.* vol. ii.
[3] Caledonian *Hort. Trans.* vol. ii.
[4] At Duddingston House, Edinburgh, in 1790; Dalry, 1795; Stoke Newington, Middlesex, in 1789. Adams and Co. potters, London, have sent them to various parts of England for hothouses during the last twenty years. Their use is described for *serres à fruits* in *Encyc. Méthod.* and *N. Dict. Œconomique*, Paris, an ix. See also Kirchner's *Practische Anleitung für Gartenkunst*, &c. Leipsig 1796.

Sir George Mackenzie has lately[1] suggested a plan of heating hothouses by an open fire place, built within and near the centre of the house, and with flues proceeding from it towards each end, &c. Sir G. is sanguine as to the success of this notion, and it must be confessed there is something social and comfortable in the idea of seeing one's plants surrounding a bright fire; but it may be doubted whether the local force of this radiating heat, its drying effect, and the dust which is thrown out by the best (even Raffele's) grates, would not counterbalance any advantage which this plan may possess in other respects. The immense conservatory attached to the palace of Taurida at Petersburgh is heated nearly in this way; but as it contains chiefly orange trees[2], and as wood is the fuel made use of, one can hardly judge from it of the effects that would be produced by coal fires among vines or tender exotics in this country.

The original construction of furnaces has been somewhat improved, by hollow bars to promote durability[3]; by double doors to the fuel-chamber, so as to prevent any air from being drawn in along with the smoke, that has not by entering through the ash pit door passed through the fuel and become heated[4]; and by a door to the ash pit, and a damper near the chimney top, by shutting either of which when the fuel is thoroughly ignited, the hot air is stagnated in the flues, which thereby remain much longer in a state to give out heat to the house, than would otherwise be the case.

Various attempts have been made to consume the smoke in hothouse furnaces, so as to obtain more heat from the fuel, and by keeping their inner surface free from soot, not only to prevent the neces-

---

[1] Caledonian *Hort. Trans.* vol. ii.

[2] The orange is particularly hardy. Quintinye (*Jardins Fruitiers*) says they require little or no heat in France; and Humboldt observes (*De Distributione geographica Plantarum*, Paris 1816, p. 158), that though the orange requires at an average in the open air 17 degrees (64° of Fahrenheit), yet it will resist a cold of 7 (45° of Fahr.) if it last only a few hours at a time.

[3] Bradley's Patent, see *Repertory of Arts*, vol. xii. New Series.

[4] Count Rumford first introduced double doors to hothouse furnaces.

sity of cleaning the flues, but to render their capacity of imbibing warmth from the current of heated air at all times equal. Wherever a white heat is constantly produced, there can be no difficulty in burning the smoke; but as hothouse fires are generally half the day either extinguished or nearly so, it may be pronounced as impracticable to produce any scheme that shall completely effect this purpose. There are however two modes, which approach perhaps as near to the attainment of this desirable object, as the above circumstance will admit of; the one is by the Marquis de Chabannes[1], and the other by Mr. Robertson[2]. In both the fuel is supplied from a hopper placed over the furnace; but that of Robertson has an air valve which renders the consumption of the smoke more complete than in those of Chabannes, which indeed are more calculated for dwelling-houses. Hopper furnaces have but in very few instances been tried in hothouses[3]; but I have little doubt of their being found real improvements, and especially if connected with the regulating apparatus already repeatedly mentioned[4].

Mr. Nicol[5], rather than run any risk from new plans of furnaces, or any improved œconomy of heat and fuel, recommends a large fuel-chamber, and the fire to be well heaped up with ashes at night, so as to keep up a constant circulation of smoke in the flues till the morning. And considering that whenever any accident happens to the house through the carelessness of the attendant, the blame is without fail attributed to the new plan, whatever that may be, this recommendation may be considered as of practical utility.

---

[1] *Explanation of a New Method*, &c. p. 21, in which the *calore fumivore* is described.

[2] Rees's *Cyclopedia*, art. Steam.

[3] A hopper furnace joined to a boiler is described by Mr. McNaught in Buchannan's *Treatise on Heating, &c. by Steam*, p. 197; but the most improved plan which I have seen for a furnace and boiler is that adopted by Mr. Fraser at the Royal Gardens at Kensington.

[4] There are various ingenious plans for consuming the smoke in grates by Franklin, Cutler and Co., Begbie and Dickson, Hawkins, and some others, attended with different degrees of success. See *Repertory of Arts*.

[5] *Forcing Gardener*, 3d edit.

. Justice, Bénard, Weston, and Dr. Anderson have proposed using lamps for supplying heat; but it is evident their use for that purpose must be very limited.

VENTILATION has hitherto been very imperfectly performed in hothouses, especially during the winter season, and in close foggy weather. Boerhaave, Linnæus, and Adanson made complaints on this head in their times; and an excellent practical gardener (Mr. Mean) in the last edition of Abercrombie's *Practical Gardener* just published states that " a good mode of ventilation is still a desideratum." Linnæus caused a stove to be erected in the centre of his Caldarium at Upsal, in order by occasional fires to purify the air of the house when the severity of the weather did not admit opening the sashes. The Dutch generally used their back sheds as reservoirs of temperate air, to be interchanged with that of the house by means of doors and other apertures in the partition, or, as it is here generally termed, the back wall. Quintinye and the editor of the third edition of *La Nouvelle Maison rustique* propose large porches or antechambers at each end of the house for similar purposes, the doors to which might act as fans every time any person entered the house[1], or the constant admission of heated air by means of Gouger's fire-places[2], which act much in the same way as the mode of ventilation adopted by Sir Humphry Davy in the House of Lords.

Hales proposes using the same machine which he applied so suc-

---

[1] *Chaque fois qu'on entrera, cette antichambre, par laquelle on puisse passer pour entrer dans la serre, se fournira d'air nouveau; et ouvrant après la porte de cette antichambre qui donne dans la serre, l'air de cette antichambre se mêlant avec celui de la serre qui est usé, lui donnera les parties nécessaires qui contribueront à la végétation et à l'acroissement des plantes.* —La Nouvelle Maison rustique, Rouen 1768, tom. ii. p. 14.

[2] *On peut pourtant faire usage des chéminées inventées par M. Gouger, dont l'avantage est qu'il entre sans cesse dans la serre, de l'air nouveau également échauffé, et que l'air qui y est renfermé en sert aussi continuellement, &c.*—Ibid. tom. ii. p. 15.

cessfully to ships [1], of which Bradley takes notice, and offers some additional hints as to its application. Dr. Anderson, however, has treated the subject most at length. He proposes reservoirs under or adjoining the house, to be filled with the superfluous heated air generated by the sun in the day-time, and to be used as occasion might require both for the purposes of ventilation and heating. "For the purpose of agitating the air of the house at pleasure, without the necessity of introducing air from without," he proposes to place a fan like that of a winnowing-machine in a cylinder so arranged as to "suck up air from any part of the house at pleasure", or if desirable from without, and "spout it out on any other part of the house with a greater or lesser degree of violence." Dr. Anderson's ideas on the subject of hot-houses were unfortunately never systematized and reduced to practice; though all of them admit of adoption under certain circumstances. His treatise on the patent hothouse is replete with the most ingenious ideas and reasonings, which, as is too often the case, will probably long remain hid till called forth by some pressing necessity, or individual interest.

Mr. Stuart in the Specification of his patent does not propose to agitate the air of the house, but to refresh and cool it down to the requisite degree, by admitting air through tubes, which commence with a funnel or trumpet mouth on the surface of the ground, outside the house, and end in a perforated plate covered with a regulating valve near the upper part of the inside of the house. The light wasted air is allowed to escape by tubes commencing at different heights from the floor, and terminating outside the roof. In this arrangement there does not appear a sufficiently powerful and active principle of motion; for no fluid is so sluggish as air.

Mr. Strutt of Derby has adopted a plan in ventilating his house which merits adoption in many cases. A tube with a funnel mouth,

---

[1] *On Ventilation*, London 1743, p. 24.

contrived to turn to the wind, commences one hundred yards from, and is conducted under ground to, the house; this supplies temperate air in winter and cool air in summer to all the different apartments. A tube on the roof, with a funnel contrived to turn with the wind, draws off or admits the escape of the wasted air from the different apartments. The same plan is used in the Derby Infirmary. In Mr. Strutt's house, the air on its introduction in the ground floor is heated by flues under the different floors of the first story. The whole arrangement in regard to heating and ventilating, no less than as to the fitting up of the kitchen and offices, is unique, and is, or was in 1811, the most complete in England.

The Marquis de Chabannes' principle of ventilation for private houses, and which he proposes to adopt also in hothouses, bears a near resemblance to Mr. Strutt's. He places a ventilator, which he calls an air pump, at the top of the house, to draw off by means of tubes communicating with the cielings of all the rooms in the house, the rarefied air; and at the bottom of the house he has a recipient or room, which in winter may be filled with hot air, and in summer with cold air, also communicating by tubes with the lower part of all the rooms. The tubes are of course furnished with valves, so that the temperature of each room may be regulated at pleasure. The air pump is kept in motion by wind, or by the smoke of the kitchen chimney after the manner of a smoke jack. It is evident that, as the air pump draws off the air, its place must be supplied from the tubes communicating with the lower recipient, unless the windows or doors are open. This arrangement certainly admits of modification, so as both to serve for heating and ventilating hothouses; but the heat produced from hot water or steam being so greatly preferable to that produced directly from ignited fuel, and the action of the air pump, when there may be little or no wind or smoke, being rather doubtful, I am inclined to think a greater degree of perfection is to be expected from the mode proposed by Mr. Benford Deacon, with the improvements of which that mode is susceptible.

For warming and ventilating, Mr. Deacon[1] heats his air in boxes or chests of highly-glazed pottery tubes, or in boxes of tubes, or, double plates, or cellular masses of cast iron, immersed in a vessel of boiling water. To convey this air to the house, he employs a fan fixed in a semi-cylindrical machine, placed in the lower part of, or any where near, the house. With this machine he draws up the air of the atmosphere, forces it through the box of immersed tubes, where it receives the requisite degree of warmth or coolness, into a main communicating by tubes with the different rooms to be heated and ventilated. In ordinary cases, the fan-machine may be kept in motion by a jack or other similar engine; on a large scale, as for heating or cooling churches, &c. by manual labour. For cooling and ventilating, the air is drawn through a dry drain, or from a cool cellar, and the box of tubes is immersed in cold water, &c.

By distributing the conducting tubes under the floor, or even under the paths only, of a hothouse, and perforating them so as the heated air might rise as equally as possible, or by using tubes of canvass or woollen netting, and by leaving unputtied the interstices between the panes of glass; a very simple and, as it appears to me, a very perfect mode of heating and ventilation would be produced. It might of course be regulated at pleasure, and used either with or without the aid of smoke flues or steam tubes. In a large range, the boxes of tubes for heating the air might be immersed in steam, under or behind each house; and one fan, and one fire and boiler, erected in a centrical situation, might produce the whole effect. The arrangement would be such, that if by accident or want of fuel the fire got low, (though with a hopper furnace this could hardly happen,) then the motion of the fans depending on the force of the steam, the quantity of air driven through the box of tubes would be lessened in pro-

---

[1] Specification of Patent 1812. These machines, which the inventor calls Æolians, are erected and answering the proposed ends at the Old Bailey, Albion Tavern, and Valpy's Printing-office. One will shortly be erected in a greenhouse at Streatham.

portion, so that there could be no chance of cold air being introduced through the fans continuing to operate when the water was cold or the steam off. I have no hesitation in risking an opinion, that with the joint use of steam, this Æolian apparatus, and Mr. Kewley's regulator, a climate might be produced more perfect than any in nature, which would not only greatly improve the size and flavour of fruits, and the health and beauty of exotic plants, but might be of some importance in pneumatic medicine[1].

But though the last plan merits adoption where perfection is aimed at, the present state of horticultural architecture, advanced as it is, will not in many cases permit of a system of ventilation so refined. The following plan, therefore, is submitted as adapted to general purposes; and which, excepting the introduction of glass tubes, differs little from the mode successfully practised by the Dutch, a nation to whom we owe in a great degree our taste for, as well as knowledge in, culinary gardening.

Form a porch at each end of the house, a vault under it, or a shed behind it, of the same length as the glass, as in PL. V. *Fig*. 1. Let the back wall as in *Fig*. 3 have three tiers of windows or horizontal openings; the upper tier above the roof of the back shed, the lower tier on a level with the ground, and the middle tier under the upper angle of the back shed roof. These windows may be either boards arranged as Venetian blinds; or, glass windows hung with pulleys and weights; or large valves turning on pivots may serve instead of sashes. Form openings in the front wall of the hothouse and back wall of the shed, either glazed or boarded; and over all the outer openings stretch haircloth or wire gauze, to keep out winged insects, and to

---

[1] Dr. Adams, in the London *Medical Journal* about fifteen years ago, seems to have been the first who suggested the idea of constructing buildings of a graduated temperature for the benefit of persons of weak lungs. Subsequently Dr. Pearson and Dr. Buxton have attempted to carry the idea into practice in spacious apartments (*Phil. Mag.* 1813); and Dr. Kentish in 1813 proposed the establishment at Clifton of a sort of hothouse for invalids, to be called a Madeira House, which, however, has not yet been carried into effect.

soften or divide the air as it enters the house. This construction formed, I need not describe the modes of creating a current, either to interchange the air of the shed with that of the house; to allow the air of the house to escape by the upper windows, and to supply its place with that in the back sheds; or to form a general ventilation by the free admission of the open air.

But there are periods when it may become requisite to admit a small quantity of air in order to refresh the atmosphere of the house, when the upper tier of windows cannot be opened. This is to be effected by means of perpendicular glass tubes, or glazed grooves or recesses in the back wall, communicating at the bottom of the wall with a tube, which tube must be conducted across and touching the flue or steam pipe, so as to derive heat from it, and thence either outside the house or to the back shed, there terminating in a funnel mouth situated a foot or eighteen inches lower than where it crosses the flue. Such tubes may be formed of earthen ware. The perpendicular glazed groove should be continued from its junction with the other at the floor to the upper part of the back wall, and there terminate in a pane of tinned iron pierced with holes, or a piece of wire gauze; and in either case it may be covered with a valve. It is evident that the only time when such an arrangement will not pour down abundance of fresh air on that of the house will be when the valves are shut, when the sun does not shine, and when there is no heat in the flues; for the heat of the flue by rarefying the air in the earthen tube, and the rays of the sun by rarefying that in the glazed groove, will produce motion whenever the fires are lighted or the sun shines, according to the power of the existing causes. Distributive tin tubes might readily be conducted from these glazed grooves down the rafters, if thought requisite; and in houses glazed on all sides, where of course glazed grooves could not be used, tin tubes glazed on one side might be introduced (placing the glazed side next the sun) either among the plants on the stage or under the pendent trellis, or in various other situations, so as perfectly to effect the object in view. They might even be constructed outside the house, where an outer curtain was used. The air introduced by these tubes would produce in the house an excess or overplus, which might either be let off by valves in the upper part of the back wall or roof, or left to escape by the crannies that necessarily exist in every house, and by the unglazed laps of the glass[1].

Artificial regulation. Some attempts have been made with a view to this object; but, with the exception of Mr. Kewley's, they are so imperfect as not to require enumeration[2].

The most beautiful and ingenious machine which has hitherto been proposed for the improvement of horticulture is the " Artificial gardener" invented by Mr. Kewley. The object of this machine is to regulate the temperature of every description of hothouse or frame, and is equally applicable to dwelling-houses for the same purpose. A thermometer is the first mover; it is placed within the atmosphere to be regulated, and the rest of the machinery fixed within or outside the house, and either near or at a convenient distance. The rising and falling of the thermometer operate on clock work; this last raises the plug of an elevated cistern, which communicating by a pipe with a cylinder and piston, raises the latter, and thus gives the power which it may easily be conceived is applicable to opening the sashes of the hothouse or hotbed, the valves or dampers of flues and steam tubes, &c. None of these machines have yet been erected in a hothouse near London; but Mr. Kewley tried one upwards of two years in his

---

[1] By forming such glazed grooves in the south elevations of dwelling-houses, and causing them to communicate either with the cielings of apartments to draw off wasted air, with cellars or dry drains to introduce fresh cool air, or with damp floors or partitions so as to prevent the dry rot, I venture to assert that a more powerful ventilation would be produced during sunshine than could be effected by any other means equally simple and œconomical, and so little liable to go out of repair.

[2] Mr. Barnstaple in 1790 adopted in the roof of a vinery, panes of glass suspended by an axle a little to one side of their centre. *Repertory of Arts,* vol. vii. Dr. Anderson in 1801 tied a flaccid bladder to valves for the same purpose. *Patent Hothouse.* Both answered the end, but in a very slight degree.

own garden in the Isle of Man, and has one in constant use for regulating the temperature of his apartments at his present residence[1]. This machine has been shown to Sir Joseph Banks, who thinks it will answer the purposed end; and I need not inform my reader of the value of the opinion of one so eminently qualified to judge, and whose extensive observation and experience have enabled him to augur of new inventions with such certainty that, as Sir Humphry Davy has remarked, it may be considered in him a sort of intuitive faculty[2].

The importance of tradesman-like workmanship, or sufficient EXECUTION, has been already noticed. The remarks to be submitted on this subject relate chiefly to those variations of construction which I purpose introducing in hothouses.

In the *masonry* of hothouses particular attention should be paid to the foundations. A very common cause of decay is rents and settlements in the front wall, which of course receives the greater weight and thrust of the roof. The foundations of these walls ought to be deeper than usual, because the ground is liable in the course of cultivation to be stirred two or three feet deep; and the wall does not generally rest on its whole base, but on piers at certain distances, in order to admit the spreading of the roots, &c. Where rafters or uprights are used, I should recommend a pier under each, fourteen inches square under ground, and above ground of smaller dimensions, according to the weight to be supported. Instead of an arch from pier to pier, it will, in all cases where air is to be admitted by openings in the front wall, be preferable to employ stone imposts, and also to have that part of the pier which is above ground of one stone nine or twelve inches square, according to circumstances: see PL. X. *Figs.* 1 and 2. The object of this arrangement is to increase the pasturage of the

---

[1] No. 7, Providence Buildings, New Kent Road. As soon as the machines are ready for sale, one will be erected here for the inspection of my friends.

[2] In a Lecture at the Royal Institution, speaking of the tannin found in terra Japonica.

roots at *a, a*, and the opening for admitting air at *b, b, Fig.* 1 ; and by having the stones properly rabbeted, to render wooden frames for the shutters of these openings, or wall plates for the rafters or astragals to rest on, unnecessary. The exact form of the upper surface of the wall plate must depend on the sort of rafter or astragal to be fixed on it. In general it should be such as will deliver outwards into a light gutter suspended from the stone, all the water of condensation which may run down the rafters or astragals.

In regard to the sort of stone to be used, each district has its local facilities for that material; but where there is not a good stone near the spot, and water carriage is not far distant, I should recommend a stone which in point of durability and strength surpasses the Portland ; and differs from it chiefly in having more sand in its composition, and being of a yellowish colour. This stone is to be had in great abundance from Colallo in Fifeshire, and may be worked there to any form, and laid down in London so as to come considerably cheaper than Portland stone[1].

The doors and openings for ventilation in the other walls should also have their sills, cheeks and lintels, of stone, properly rabbeted, so as there may be no wood-work required but for the shutters or doors.

Where pavement is used, I should recommend, as preferable to any pavement I have seen, the Arbroath flag-stone. It may be had in very large masses, which is a great advantage; and is so little absorbent of moisture, that even when laid on damp ground it always appears dry and comfortable.

The *wood-work* of hothouses such as I recommend, where improve-

---

[1] It has been extensively used in the Penitentiary at Millbank, and various other places; and specimens may be seen at Mr. Stoddart's, Strand. The present proprietor of this invaluable quarry, Mr. F. Braidwood of Edinburgh, has not yet been able to make it sufficiently known; in doing which he of course experiences great opposition from the proprietors and advocates of Portland stone. Excellent specimens of this stone, and also of the Arbroath pavement, may be seen in the greenhouse erected here (Bayswater) already referred to.

ment is an object[1], will be very trifling, and consist chiefly of shutters to the openings for ventilation doors, and fittings up for the back sheds. Sometimes also the outer frames of iron sashes are proposed to be formed of wood. In all cases, to promote duration, the wood-work of hothouses should be first fitted together, then taken asunder and painted two or three times with boiling tar. When dry it should be finally put together, and then painted with Le Souff's "anticorrosion," which after twenty years experience has been found the most durable paint for hothouses[2].

The *metallic work* requires particular care in the execution so as to prevent rust. I have already mentioned a necessary precaution for that purpose (p. 45), and may here add, that where cast iron is to be used as wall plating, or in masses to be inserted in the ground, in walls, or used as tanks or cisterns, the composition with which Mr. Dickenson (inventor of the iron buoys) coats his patent iron casks will be found a desirable addition.

As the weight of cast iron rafters, as hitherto adopted in hothouses, has been an objection to their use, I shall here give some forms which will render them nearly or entirely as light as wood, with all the advantages (and some additional ones) of the heavy rafters of which there are sections in Pl. VIII. *Fig.* 7.

1. Supposing the rafter intended for a common sloping roof for two tiers of sashes, both to slide, viz. the upper sashes to slide down, and the lower ones to slide up or down at pleasure; then *Fig.* 1, Pl. IX. will represent a side view of such a rafter as cast, and before it has received the requisite fittings up. It may either be cast in one length, to be screwed together at *a, a,* or in four lengths, and joined at *b, a, b.*

Fig. 2 is a side view of the same rafter fitted with rollers, *d, d,*

---

[1] It sometimes happens that an architect in his employer's instructions is forbid to introduce any plan not in use in the neighbourhood, or which does not correspond with a house already erected, &c. &c.; in which case, plans in general use must be resorted to.

[2] A very good proof of this may be seen in Miller and Sweet's Nursery, Bristol, and in some very neat wooden houses which they have erected at an adjoining villa.

which turn on fixed axles for the sashes to rest on instead of the usual rabbet, and which serve at the same time to lessen the friction when the sashes are in motion. The short cylindrical pieces, c, c, are cast apart, with gudgeons to fit small sockets, which sockets, with the cylinders fitted in, are screwed to the upper and lower bars of the rafter. The use of these vertical cylinders is to lessen the friction on the sides of the sashes when they are in motion.

Fig. 3 is a view of the same rafter completely fitted up, and with the sashes in their places.

> e..f is a gutter suspended from the under edge of the rafter, to collect any water which may enter in the interstices between the sashes and rafter. This gutter may be formed of tinned iron, leather, or varnished *papier maché*; and as it rests on the forked ends of the wire suspenders, g, it may be taken out and put in at pleasure.
>
> h. Transverse rods to retain the rafters on edge and at equal distances, and also to keep down the sashes.

Supposing this rafter to be twenty feet in length, and the bars at an average three quarters of an inch square, it will weigh one hundred and three quarters, which at the present London prices will cost, including the fittings up, about 2l. 10s. With regard to the strength of such a rafter, a sufficient number of experiments have not yet been made on cast iron[1] to admit of a correct estimate; but there can be no doubt of its supporting ten hundred weight, or double the weight of the sashes which would bear on it, even if laid in a horizontal position and unaided by supports at any part between the two ends. By doubling the number of braces its strength will be increased by nearly one third part, and by placing it in an inclined position, like the sloping roof of a hothouse, every one knows that the weight it will bear increases as the cosine of the angle of elevation diminishes. The lightest wooden rafter that could be made to answer the same pur-

---

[1] See Rees's *Cyclopædia*, art. Strength of Materials.

pose would require eight cubic feet of timber, which with labour at the present London prices would amount to 2*l*. 8*s*., to which must be added the expense of the rollers which would in this case be required for the sashes, the greater first cost of painting, and greater cost annually for repairs. The cast iron rafter would thus be the cheapest at first, the most durable, the most elegant, and it would not throw above one third of the shadow of the other on the glass.

2. Supposing the width of the house the same, and that it were (as in most cases it is) desirable that the one sash should move up, and the other down; then *Fig. 4* will represent a side view of such a rafter with the sashes in their places.

 a. An iron plate, which projects from the bottom rail of the upper sash over the upper rail of the lower sash, to carry off the wet.

 b. A projecting plate, for the same purpose, to throw off the water at the upper angle of the back wall.

 c. Transverse rods to fix the rafters and retain the sashes. When it is desirable to open them further, they can be lifted up and tilted, or taken entirely off. This rafter would be equally strong, and one fourth cheaper than the other.

Mr. Timmins[1] proposes a very neat mode of forming metallic rafters, by casing plates of cast or wrought iron with thin copper, which, if it were desirable to continue the old form of rafters, might in many cases be adopted with advantage, the precaution of tinning the copper being duly attended to before introduced in houses where grapes were grown. But curved rafters and convex roof promise so many

---

[1] Specification of Patent for improvements in hothouses, March 1813. A very elegant house by Mr. Timmins is erected in Mr. Loddige's Nursery, which in point of lightness and tradesman-like workmanship surpasses any I have seen. Mr. Timmins generally tins his copper. Mr. Jorden, in his patent house erected for public inspection in the Union Nursery, King's Road, has used a light rafter; but as only a small part of the roof of that house is moveable, it became an easy matter to omit superfluous strength. The water escape bars and grooves in that house are neat and ingenious.

advantages over straight rafters and upright and sloping glass, that they will soon in all probability take place of every other plan.

Though curved rafters may be placed at double the distance of the common sort, and consequently must sustain double their weight, yet they may be made still lighter than those just described. In short, an astragal of wrought iron drawn of double the usual size, would form a sufficiently strong rafter for all the ordinary purposes of convex roofs.

Fig. 3, Pl. X., exhibits three different rafters of cast iron, each twenty-five feet long and placed six feet asunder, in all of which the under rib or rod, *a...b*, with or without a water gutter attached to it, is intended to support a vine. If the house were narrower,—that is, if the back wall were in the situation of the perpendicular lines, *c, d,* or *e,—*, then of course the rafter would be made lighter; and if wider, as for such houses as that in Pl. IV., stronger, and the braces differently arranged. Any one who has studied with attention the roof of the *Halle au blé* in Paris, need not be told that where a curve is the form given there is no known limit to roofs of this description.

Figs. 4 and 5 are sections of the rafter, showing different modes of attaching wires for the vines, and of placing the sashes, &c.

The sort of valvular shutters before described may be seen at *f, f, f,* in *Fig.* 3, and the situation of a wire cloth to exclude tempests and insects at *g, g*. The opening, *h,* looking into the back shed of temperate air, does not require this sort of protection. In winter these wire cloths might be covered with woollen netting, by which means Mr. Kewley's regulator might be allowed to open not only the valves communicating with the back shed, but even the others, at all seasons of the year.

In this figure the outer curtain is contained in a slated box serving as coping to the back wall; by observing the section of which it will readily be conceived how the one breadth of curtain will overlap the other when let down.

This house is supposed to be heated by steam with smoke flues in the back wall, merely to exhaust in the brickwork a part of what heat may escape from the boiler, and thus to temperate the reserve air in the back shed.

Metallic sashes. One of the greatest improvements in this department of execution consists in the adoption of metallic bars or astragals, instead of the cumbrous wooden ones used when hothouses were first introduced. Adanson is the earliest author who recommends them (in 1763), and they have been occasionally used in this country since, and even before Adanson's time, but chiefly since 1783[1]. The principal metals used are iron, copper, and pewter.

Cast iron astragals and frames are in use for windows of manufactories and private houses, but from their weight and clumsiness are much less suitable for hothouses than those of wrought iron. Wrought iron astragals are commonly made in two parts, the moulding and hoop, or in architectural language the band and astragal (see *a* and *b*, Fig. 7, Pl. X.). These are then hammered together, and make a very neat and durable bar or astragal[2]. I have succeeded in getting them drawn in one solid body through moulds, which renders them stronger, better adapted for curved work, and, there being less labour, somewhat cheaper[3]. Tinning such astragals is of course a great improvement, and should never be neglected where perfection is aimed at.

Wrought iron hoops or bands, tinned and soldered to astragals[4] or other mouldings of pewter, or any such composition of tin and lead in which brass or zinc forms a small proportion, form very light and durable bars, and which are not liable to rust, at least on the

---

[1] Mr. Playfair of Howland-street, engineer, in 1783; Mr. Underwood, plumber and glazier, in 1782; and Mr. Nash, glazier, about the same time,—were chiefly instrumental in their introduction. Mr. Nash used copper, Mr. Underwood pewter on iron hoops and wires, and Mr. Playfair any ductile metal according to circumstances.

[2] Chiefly used by Mr. Cruikshanks, sash-manufacturer, Gerrard-street.

[3] For the advantages of this astragal see page 35. *Astragal* and *bar* I use synonymously

[4] *Repertory of Arts*, vol. vii.

[5] Chiefly used by Messrs. Doyle, Underwood, and Co. Holborn.

(79)

inner surface of the sash (see *a* and *b*, Fig. 8, Pl. X.). From the difference, however, between the expansive powers of the iron rabbet or band and the pewter moulding, change of temperature may occasion their twisting, and even effect their separation; to prevent which the hoop should be burnt in (as the term is), the edge to which the moulding is to be attached being previously serrated and beat back; and a proper mould formed, into which it may be fixed upright, and the melted metal run in (see Fig. 9, *a*, *b*, *c*, and *d*, Pl. X.).

Astragals or bars of sheet copper drawn through moulds to different patterns have been long in use, and among others by Playfair and Nash already mentioned[1]. For straight work, and especially for upright glass, they form a very neat astragal; but they are unsuitable for curved work, and in any form are more expensive than either iron or composition bars, having at the same time the additional disadvantage of producing verdigrise through any accidental neglect of painting, and the presence of carbonic acid gas or ammonia. For this reason they should at all events never be used in hotbed frames, where both these gases rise abundantly from the dung, bark, or other putrescent matters. Of course the very idea of danger is ridiculed, and the circumstance of any families having been injured by copper stoutly denied, by the tradesmen who manufacture articles from this metal[2].

Astragals wholly of pewter or other composition, cast or drawn

---

[1] At present Mr. Timmins and Mr. Jorden, both of Birmingham, are the principal manufacturers of copper bars and sashes.

[2] A new source of danger to life appears to have been introduced by modern refinement. A Bath paper recently announced the death of Mrs. A. Parnell, aged 56, from eating cucumbers raised by sheet copper reflectors. She died in about three hours after eating of them. It is probable that these cucumbers became strongly impregnated with oxide (subcarbonate) of copper, from the moisture with which the plates must be always covered, being charged with the oxide (subcarbonate) of this metal, formed by the action of the oxygen and the carbonic acid of the atmosphere on the plates; and then falling on and being absorbed by the plants beneath. —*Lond. Med. Repository*, vol. iv. p. 255.

through moulds, or formed of brass, eldorado metal, &c. are more adapted for shop fronts and church windows than for hothouses.

The frames of sashes where they are not to slide may be made of metal, either of hollow copper[1] or hollow iron, or of cast iron, or by wrought iron drawn to the form of *Fig.* 6, PL. X, and tinned, which is the description of styles and rails I purpose using for the hinged sashes in curved roofs.

Fitting in the astragals to the outer frames may seem so simple a process as not to deserve mentioning. But when the frames are of wood it is of the utmost importance. The common and I may say universal mode is to rabbet the styles, and insert the ends of the astragals in the top and bottom bar; the consequence of which is, that one grand advantage of metallic astragals, the durability of hothouse sashes, is as completely lost as if the whole sash were made of wood; and the greater number of copper and iron houses which have been erected within these few years at an increased expense with the bearing rafters and outer frames of wood, and the astragals only of metal, will not be found more durable, *ceteris paribus*, than the less costly, though certainly less elegant houses in the old style, and formed of wood alone. The reason is as follows.

Wooden sash-frames generally decay first at the angles where they are framed together by tenon and mortise: when decay takes place there, it matters not whether they are fitted in with metallic or wooden astragals, as the whole sash must be taken to pieces and renewed. It is true that in theory the metallic astragals may be fitted or inserted in a new wooden frame, but in practice the thing is never done. Much of the glass is destroyed in unglazing, and the astragals are generally broken off at the ends so as to become too short for a new frame. This is particularly the case with frames filled in with copper astragals, which are generally let into notches; but less so

---

[1] As described by Mr. Timmins in his Specification already referred to.

with the iron astragals of Mr. Cruikshanks and Messrs. Doyle and Underwood, which are generally screwed to the frames[1].

The method which I have used extensively, and which I should recommend in every case, is as follows:—Instead of rabbeting the sash, apply a half metallic bar with rabbet and half moulding to each of the two sides and top rail of the sash, and an entire moulding or small bar of iron to the bottom rail. These being fitted to the inside of the wooden frame, are then to be taken out and riveted together, thus forming a metallic frame, to which the astragals and bearing bars are to be riveted. This metallic frame so filled in is then to be screwed to the wooden frame. Of course, when the latter rots, the former, by unscrewing from six to ten screws, can be taken out with the glass entire, and placed within a new frame of wood at a mere trifle of expense. In this way, one set of astragals may endure against three or four sets of wooden frames. The convenience of carriage also, though a trifling advantage, deserves to be mentioned; for these inner frames, occupying so little room, may be made of any shape, and sent glazed or unglazed to the most distant parts of the empire. A proprietor in a remote district may thus choose his design from his gardener or some book, employ his own carpenter to make the rough or plainest work, and get his sashes, which form the grand article of difficulty and expense, from a source where he can calculate on receiving tradesman-like goods.

The mouldings of astragals have been varied, not only according to taste or fancy, but for purposes of utility.

Fig. 10, Pl. X. is a section of what Mr. Jorden calls his water escape bar.

Fig. 11 is one which I have used for hotbed lights, made of three tinned hoops riveted together.

---

[1] This may be seen in three frames procured from Messrs. Jorden, Cruikshanks, and Doyle and Co. made in 1816, and forming part of the variety of patterns which compose the greenhouse at Bayswater before mentioned.

Fig. 12 shows the manner in which a tinned hoop may be bent and applied to the underside of a solid iron astragal; some of which I have used in ridge and furrow glazing. Where the lap used is such as to throw the water to the astragal, and the roof is flat, any of these forms may be found useful; but I may here repeat, that wherever an outer curtain is used condensation will very rarely take place.

The bearing bars of sashes, or those on which long astragals are caused to rest, between the top and bottom rails, and with which they are kept steady, in regard to breadth, ought to be so formed and placed as to effect these objects without interrupting the course of the water of condensation in its progress down the mouldings of the astragals.

Fig. 13, Pl. X. is a very good form for this purpose; *Fig.* 14 is the form for which Mr. Jorden has taken out a patent; but *Fig.* 15 is by much the best mode, as it not only strengthens the astragals more than any other, but can never in any way interrupt the water of condensation. In all cases it will be an improvement not to fix these bars directly across the sash, but obliquely, so as the water which condenses on them may be thrown to one side, and so carried off with that on the astragals, rails, or sashes. This last mode is particularly suitable for solid iron astragals. It is due to Messrs. Timmins and Jorden to state, that they have paid more attention to water escape bars than any other hothouse builders.

Notwithstanding the permanency and lightness of metallic rafters and sashes, various cases may occur where timber will have the preference,—as for example where the ground on which the building is to be erected is held for a limited term, and where from prospective arrangements durability is less an object than present use. These cases may occur combined in the wants of a nurseryman or public gardener; and where there exists no such reason, the experience of the gardener, or prejudice of some favourite menial, (and most country gentlemen, indeed all of us, are more led by some obscure localized dependant than by reason and common sense,) may lead to the same conclusions. To promote therefore the durability of timber houses, in addition to the remarks already submitted as to the use of tar, &c. let them be formed on as light a construction as possible, and, when wide, well supported by props or pillars; the joints not held together by tenon pins, but by tenon wedges, and all the joints set, not in glue, but in white lead [1].

Glazing. Formerly the worst description of crown glass was used in hothouses; but if, as Bouguer has shown [2], one fortieth part of the light which falls perpendicularly on the clearest crystal is reflected, or does not pass through it, green glass must at least reflect or exclude one half. Œconomy in glass is therefore no œconomy, and produces effects really as disagreeable to the eye as injurious to vegetation.

The air which enters between the laps of the panes in hothouses first suggested the idea of closing these with putty, or with a lead lap similar to what is used in lattice windows. This being found to prevent the condensed dews from escaping outside the glass, gave rise at first to closing the lap partially with putty, and subsequently to different modes of cutting and disposing the panes. The principal modes are as follow:

Common hothouse glazing. Fig. 5, Pl. IX. shows the common form of pane. If the lap or projection is unputtied, its breadth may be from one quarter to three quarters of an inch; when wholly puttied, it need not project above a quarter of an inch; and when a space one inch long is left open in the centre, the projection may be half an inch. In these cases, the glass is of course placed obliquely to the plane of the rabbet which contains it.

Fragment glazing. Fig. 6 represents a mode of glazing with fragments of glass, which are generally lost or but of little use to the glass-

---

[1] This, as well as the use of tar, is practised by Mr. Pilbrough, carpenter and builder, New Milman-Street, Foundling Hospital, whom from experience I can safely recommend as an improved wooden hothouse builder.

[2] *Traité d'Optique;* and Dr. Young's *Lectures,* 35 and 39.

cutters. It is chiefly adopted by nurserymen and market gardeners for the sake of œconomy, as quantity and bulk are more their object than flavour. As the angular forms are generally brought in so as to throw the water on the astragal, the lap admits of being entirely putttied up; which is essentially necessary in cucumber frames on account of the increased number of interstices, which would otherwise cool too rapidly their small volume of heated air.

Common glazing with a leaden lap. The common form of pane, but placed in one plane and joined, not by the panes lapping over each other, but by the intervention of a lap of lead, *a*, which projects over them reciprocally on both sides. This method about twenty years ago was a good deal in use. In flat roofs it is apt to admit the wet; but when applied to ridge and furrow sashes, or to panes cut diagonally, or in the form of rhomboids, it is of considerable use.

Rhomboidal glazing. Fig. 7. This is a very good mode, especially if a metallic lap be used, as in place of leaving the condensed water to run down the glass it throws it on the astragals. It has been chiefly used by Mr. Stuart in connexion with a very ingenious metallic lap invented[1] by him; the origin of which may be recognised in the shred of lead which glaziers sometimes introduce between newly glazed panes to retain them in their places (see *b*). This lap adds greatly to the strength of hothouse glazing, and may be considered as preferable to all other modes for preserving the glass from being broken. It is generally made of copper; but in hothouses ought to be manufactured from some ductile compound of metals not obnoxious to rapid oxidation.

Perforated shield glazing. Fig. 8. This mode and that of *Fig.* 7 are obviously derived from *Fig.* 6. The interstices are puttied, excepting a space of about half an inch in the centre, to which the condensed dews are naturally thrown, and these pass to the outside of

---

[1] Specification, September 1811.

the glass. Mr. Jorden has taken out a patent for this mode, which he calls "perforated shield glazing [1]," and he states that he uses a hard putty in the interstices of the lap, in which he forms a groove for the water, &c. It has nothing to recommend it, but the novelty of its appearance; for, by the perforation in the upper part of the shield, the dexter and sinister chiefs are liable to be broken off; and by the acumination of its base, it is rendered obnoxious to the same casualty in the nombril point.

Entire shield glazing. *Fig.* 9. The shield being entire, of course where the chief of the one overlaps the base of the other, a space of double glass will be formed in the junction in the form of an isosceles triangle. This space is puttied up, excepting two openings of about half an inch each at the sides for the escape of the water, and to which it is thrown by the acumination of the inverted base of the shield. This mode is much stronger than *Fig.* 8; but the opaque triangular space gives it a heavy appearance, and in fact excludes a good deal of light. It is used by Mr. Butler, a respectable wooden hothouse builder, and may be seen in the house erected by him for Mr. Palmer at Kingston before mentioned.

Common glazing with a circular lap. *Fig.* 10. This has all the supposed advantages of *Figs.* 8 and 9, without any of their numerous disadvantages. It has been long used by Mr. Miller, a respectable glazier in Swallow-street, and may be considered for common purposes as preferable to all others with the lap half puttied; or, in connexion with an outer roofing, with the lap open.

Glazing with the circular lap reversed. *Fig.* 11. This is merely the reverse of the last mode.

Ridge and furrow glazing has been already described[2]. There are some other varieties; but as they are either well known, or unsuitable for hothouses, they do not require to be particularized.

---

[1] Specification, &c. August 1811.

[2] See page 23. These eight modes of glazing, and some other modes of less note, may be seen combined in the greenhouse and pit erected here, and frequently referred to.

There remains only to remark on the improvements which have been made in hotbeds and hotwalls.

Various gardeners have endeavoured to œconomize the stable dung generally used for HOTBEDS, by mixtures of earth, turf, ashes, sawdust, bark, &c. which might at the same time moderate and prolong its heat. For the same purpose, bundles of sticks, empty barrels, broken pots, stones, turf drains, &c. have been introduced, in forming the bed, immediately under the centre of each intended hill or group of plants. Mr. M°Phail is the first who seems to have given these practices a determinate construction, by forming compartments for the earth and plants, and surrounding them by perforated flues of masonry to which linings are from time to time applied [1]. Attempts have been made to simplify his method by substituting perforated turf-walls or walls of decayed pease sticks or faggots, instead of the flues, &c. Neatness has also been studied, by placing the frames on pillars of brick or stone [2], on perforated brick walls, and by sinking the bed of dung in a pit, and covering the linings by boards, &c. [3]

Laurence in the last edition of his Kalendar (1715) suggests the idea of putting a bottom of wire to the frames of hotbeds, and of covering it with flat tiles, and over these the earth, &c. so as to admit of the whole being lifted, and the dung stirred or renewed at pleasure. He says he has not seen it done, but merely throws it out as a hint to the ingenious. Nearly a century afterwards Mr. Weeks [4] invented his patent forcing-frame, the bottom of which is formed of wood, detached from the frame, and winds up so as to leave free access to the dung, or retain the plants at any required distance from the glass in the day time. This plan promises considerable advantages,

---

[1] M°Phail *On the Culture of the Cucumber, &c.* 2d edit. London, 1795.
[2] Beattie in Caledonian *Hort. Trans.* vol. i.
[3] Sanderson, *Ibid.* vol. ii. and Niel *On Scottish Gardens and Orchards.*
[4] Hothouse-builder, King's Road, Chelsea. See *Repertory of Arts*, vol. xiii. p. 81; and *The Forcer's Assistant*, by Edward Weeks, Chipping Norton, 1814.

and deserves trial in all private gardens where early forcing is an object.

In respect to the boxes or wooden frames, the only general improvement made in their construction is that of keying them together, instead of making permanent joints; by which means they may be taken to pieces and preserved dry, repainted, &c. when not in use[1]. Cast iron frames have been tried, but are too powerful conductors ever to answer the purpose.

With respect to the glass frames of hotbeds, Mr. Henderson[2], " in order to increase light and heat," has " adopted a construction which may be termed the triple meridian sash." The glass is raised in the manner of a pavilion roof, presenting three planes; one exposed to the east for the morning sun, another to the south for that at mid day, and a third to the afternoon's sun. Mr. Henderson built his hothouses on the same principle, with glass on all sides and their ends to the south, as in the range in the Dublin Society's gardens, near Dublin, and after seven years' trial he finds this plan answer his expectations.

I have tried one sash of this sort here, together with another in which the glass is in a semicuneiform shape, the section of the obtuse end being semicircular, which effects more completely the same object. I have also tried a sash glazed in the ridge and furrow manner, with grooves in the furrow astragals, which some excellent practical gardeners are of opinion will increase the effect of the morning and afternoon's sun, and totally prevent the water of condensation from dropping on the plants.

Various modes have been tried or suggested for supplying heat to hotbeds without the aid of dung, some of which have been hinted at; such as cast iron boxes of the same size of the hotbed, filled with hot water obtained from a distillery[3] or other manufactory, or from a hot

---

[1] Mawe's and Macdonald's *Dictionaries of Gardening*, &c.
[2] Niel *On Scottish Gardens and Orchards*, App.
[3] By the late Dr. Watt of Glasgow.

spring; by metallic reflectors to concentrate the calorific rays of the sun [1]; by collecting the sun's heat in reservoirs, &c. &c. In addition I shall suggest to the curious the idea of employing the chemical agency of calorific [2] or incanescent mixtures [3], the mechanical effect of compressing air in cast iron boxes or tubes [4], and the absorbent effects of black substances, such as troughs of pitch, powdered coal, soot, &c. during sunshine, and which shall radiate a sufficiency during night and in his absence to keep up the temperature of the air of the hotbed.

HOTWALLS seem first to have been adopted by the Duke of Rutland at Belvoir Castle, about or before 1710 [5]; since which time they have become very general in the north of England and in Scotland. In respect to the mere construction of the wall there has been little or no improvement; nor at first sight do they seem to admit of much in that respect; but numerous varieties of screens, or protections from frosts and dews, have been invented, and applied with considerable degrees of success. Frondiform branches of the evergreen fir tribe [6], straw ropes placed at regular distances [7], mats of straw, reeds, bark, or rushes [8], boards placed horizontally and perpendicularly [9], oiled paper

---

[1] *Bath Society's Papers.*

[2] Sulphuric acid and water, for example.

[3] As a certain proportion of sulphur, iron, and lime, &c.

[4] Mr. Dalton has estimated that air compressed to half its dimensions has its temperature elevated to about 50 degrees. Hence it may be inferred that a condensation equal to 1-180th of the bulk of any portion of air will raise its temperature one degree. When air is very rapidly condensed in the condenser of an air gun, it is sometimes so much heated as actually to set on fire a small portion of tow placed near the end of the barrel.—Young's *Lectures*, 39. p. 632.

[5] Laurence's *Fruit Garden Kalendar*, edit. 1718. Introd. p. 22. Switzer's *Practical Fruit Gardener*, edit. 1724, art. Wall.

[6] Niel *On Scottish Gardens and Orchards*, art. Hotwalls.

[7] J. Laird in Caledonian *Hort. Trans.* vol. i. p. 342.

[8] Edinburgh *Encyclopedia*, art. Horticulture, sect. Preserving of Blossom.

[9] Laurence in *Fruit Garden Kalendar*, &c,

frames, canvass frames, and other contrivances, have been used for this purpose; but the regular systematic construction is curtains or blinds of oiled bunting, Osnaburg or coarse woollen netting[1] attached to the projecting coping to be let down or drawn up at pleasure.

The object of hotwalls being more to mature the young wood and fruit in the autumn, and to protect the blossom from frosts in spring, than to force or procure premature vegetation, the latter object has been successfully attempted by covering the trees with boards or branches, so as to exclude the sun in the day-time, and exposing them at night. This practice is common in the north of Europe, and I would suggest from it the following idea, for very early forcing of grapes or peaches. Grow the plants or trees to be forced in pots or boxes, and retard vegetation during the whole of the summer previously to the winter you intend forcing, by keeping them in an ice-house. Take them out in the autumn or beginning of winter, say in October, after having been there twelve months, and place them in a hothouse of suitable temperature, &c. It is probable with judicious management any sort of fruit might be thus obtained from January till the usual season of forced fruits; in short, with a pinery and a large ice-house any person might thus gather ripe grapes, peaches, apricots, apples, pears, cherries, gooseberries, strawberries, &c. &c. every day in the year[2]. Whether any thing could be done in aid of this plan by employing frigorific mixtures in air-tight sheds or cel-

---

[1] Edinburgh *Encyclopædia*, art. Horticulture, sect. Preserving of Blossom.

[2] On the 20th April, 1814, there were in the hothouses of the Imperial gardens at Tzaritsina near Moscow, ripe apples, pears, cherries, plums, gooseberries, raspberries, and strawberries, and most sorts of salads, roots, legumes, &c. fit for use, such as parsley, lettuce, carrots, turnips, potatoes, pease, &c. The open ground had been covered five months with snow, and was so till about the first of May. On the evening of the 1st of June, the eve of my departure from Moscow, there was a fall of snow which covered the ground nearly two inches. If in such a climate the art of forcing is so far advanced, what may not be done in this country, where we have so much more sun during our short winter?

lars, instead of resorting to icehouses, might easily be tried; and from Professor Leslie's recent experiments with powdered granite, at very trifling expense.

I have already mentioned some of the advantages to be derived from a zig-zag wall as a common garden wall (p. 32)[1], and I have now to suggest the idea of employing a double wall of this description as a hotwall. By the double wall a vacuity would be formed capable of being either heated as one large vertical smoke chamber, or divided horizontally so as to be formed into flues, and heated in the usual way. The trees would be trained on a trellis formed by stretching wires horizontally along the wall at the distance of the thickness of two bricks, and fixed to the salient angles of the zig-zag work. The advantages of this disposition of trellis and wall would be very considerable. Independently of the advantages of a double meridian already mentioned, the heat radiated during night from the two sides of the wall in the rentrant angles would be reflected back, and prevented from escaping by the two brick sides and by the trellis forming the third side of this triangle—from the body of air contained in this triangle the flavour of the fruit will be rendered superior to that of those grown on common walls, in as much as it will approach nearer to that of standard trees which is surrounded by light and air on all sides: and from no part of the trees touching the wall no heat of the flues can ever injure them. The œconomy of this construction is also a considerable recommendation, since a double wall as above described will not require many more bricks than a nine-inch wall, whereas hotwalls are in general built twenty-four inches and

---

[1] Miller in his *Dict.*, art. Wall, and Robinson in his *Collection of Designs for Stoves, &c.*, London 1791, *description of plate* 22, mention, and at the same time disapprove of, angular walls. But as the angles in the walls to which they allude were intended to be so large as that each side might contain a trained tree, there would be no saving of materials in constructing them. These walls, indeed, both in construction and principle are radically different from the zig-zag wall; the object of the former being different exposures; that of the latter, to save expense and retain heat with the same exposure as that of a common wall.

half wide. If an extensive range of such walling were to be heated by steam, the best mode would be to leave a vacuity from the bottom to the top of the wall, and to lay one cast iron steam tube along the bottom of the vacuity. In this way, whatever might be the extent, even if the whole of the wall surrounding a garden were double, it might readily be heated from one boiler[1].

Inclined walls[2] might be built hollow by either of the three modes mentioned in a former part of these Remarks (p. 31): no more bricks would be required for every yard in length of a wall inclined to an angle of 50 degrees, than are now required for every yard of a solid fourteen-inch wall. They might be heated by steam in the manner proposed above for a hollow vertical wall, and in all cases there should be a curtain of woollen netting to be let down early in the afternoon, and pulled up only during rain and sunshine[3]. A sloping wall properly arranged would be a very excellent substitute for late forcing-houses.

---

[1] The hothouses in Messrs. Loddige's nursery now heating by steam form two parallel ranges of 500 or 600 feet each. It is intended to join these sides by ends of 200 or 300 feet each, thus forming a continuous parallelogram of glass, the whole to be heated by steam, and from one boiler. When finished it will be the most extensive thing of the sort in the world, and highly creditable to these gentlemen both in respect to design and execution. The idea of adopting steam Mr. Loddige received from Mr. Massland of Stockport, who has adopted it extensively in his hothouses, as has Mr. Knight, the President of the Horticultural Society, in a house recently erected at Downton Castle.

[2] For their advantages see Facio's work formerly referred to. As far as I have been able to learn, there are only two copies of this book in London; one in the library of the Royal Society, and the other in that of Sir Joseph Banks, to whose liberality I am indebted for the perusal of this, as well as several other scarce works referred to in these Remarks.

[3] One variety of Mr. Kewley's machine does not go so far as to regulate the temperature, but simply indicates by *sound* what ought to be done. It consists of a thermometer which rings a bell or an alarum when the mercury rises or falls to any particular degree, or at any temperature at which some operation requires to be performed by the gardener. Such a thermometer might be placed on the hotwall, and the index put to the proper degree according to the season, &c.; so as to ring for the gardener at the exact moment when the curtains are to be let down in the afternoon. A similar thermometer in the open garden might indicate the proper time to draw them up or uncover in the morning. The uses to which the forcing gar-

(92)

I consider the zig-zag garden wall, double or single, as not the least improvement suggested in these Remarks; and those who choose to adopt it in future may save themselves nearly two-thirds of the usual expense of garden walls, and have a wall better suited to their purpose. That the principle is capable of extensive application in walls and buildings of every description, will be abundantly evident to every person possessing the slightest knowledge of the principles of mechanics.

---

dener might apply these machines are numerous, and important; and the accuracy of which his operations would thus become susceptible, affords a beautiful specimen of human ingenuity and of the progress of science. A gardener might have different bells in his bed-chamber communicating with "*artificial gardeners*," or "alarum thermometers," in each of the different houses under his care, which would ring at every unwished-for fall or rise of temperature, and thus acquaint him with what was going forward or ought to be done. Even in the day-time such bells or alarums would be extremely useful; for by either having one bell in each house or hotbed, or, what would be better, one in a central situation communicating with the thermometers in the different houses, the gardener would be called from any part of the garden where he might be at work, to give air or stir the fire. A similar arrangement would be useful in dwelling-houses and manufactories, either to indicate an improper degree of heat or to warn in case of fire, &c.

THE END.

PRINTED BY RICHARD AND ARTHUR TAYLOR, SHOE-LANE.

Pl. 1

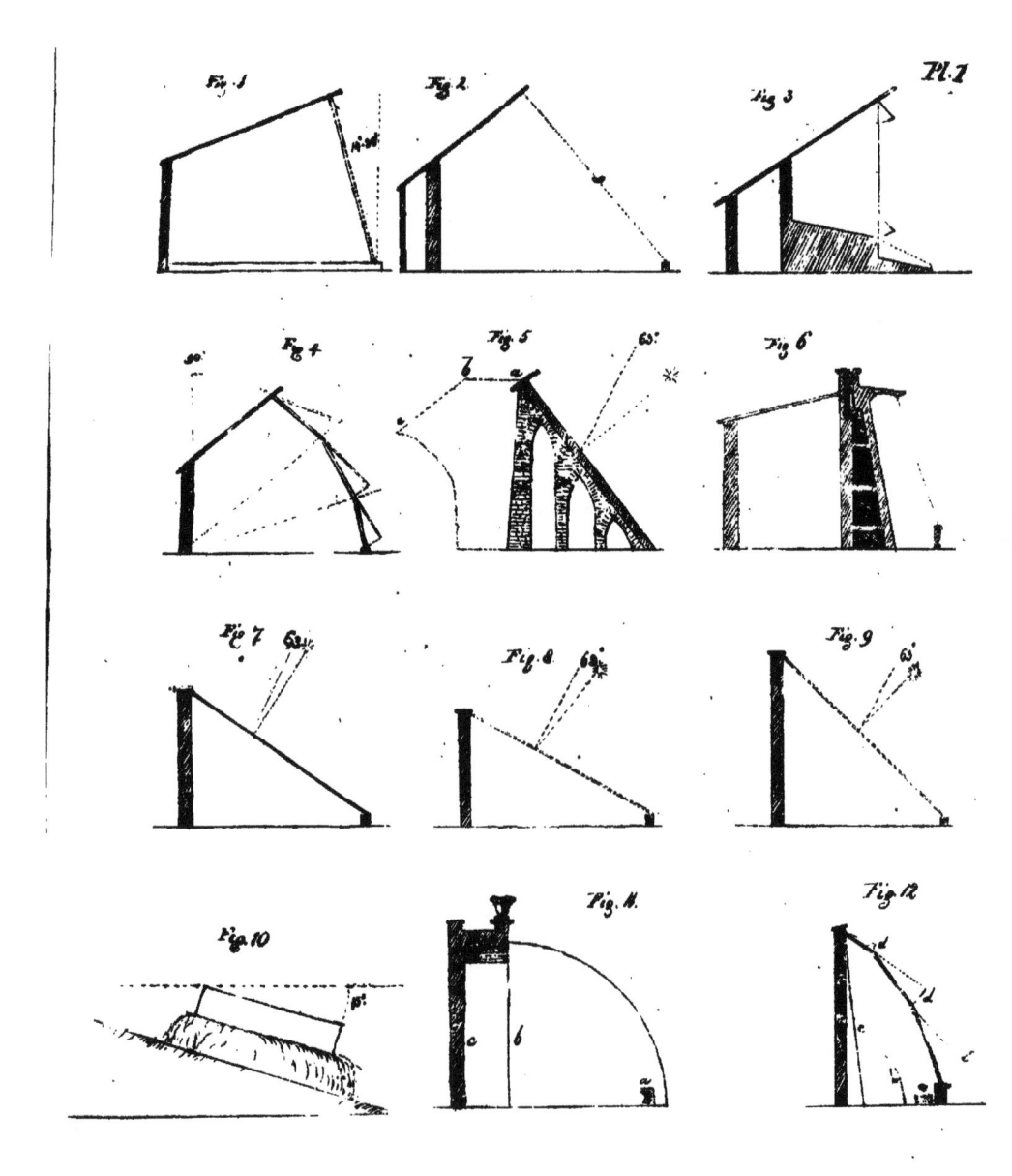

Pl. II

Fig. 5

Fig. 1

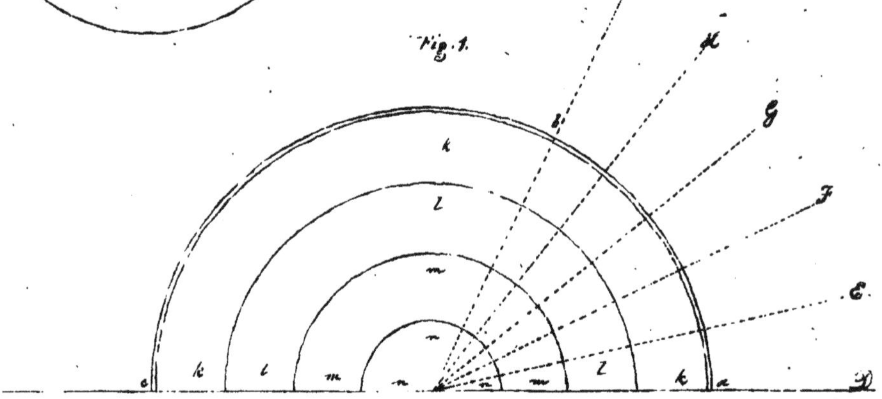

Fig. 2

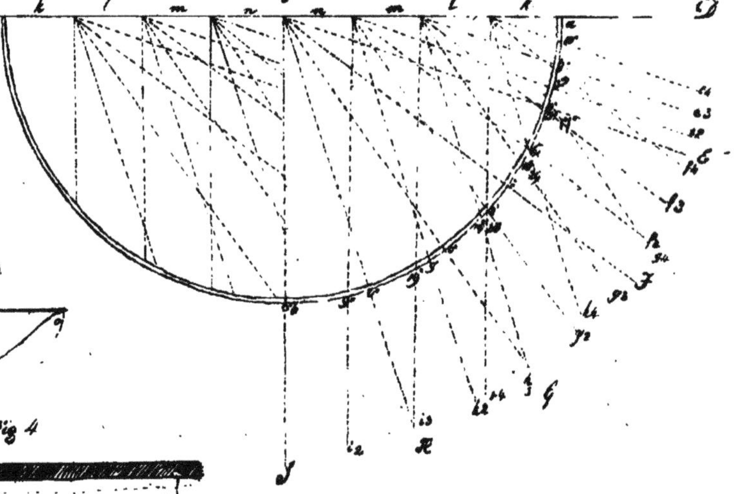

Fig. 3

Fig. 4

J. C. Loudon

Pub.d for the Repository. April 10.

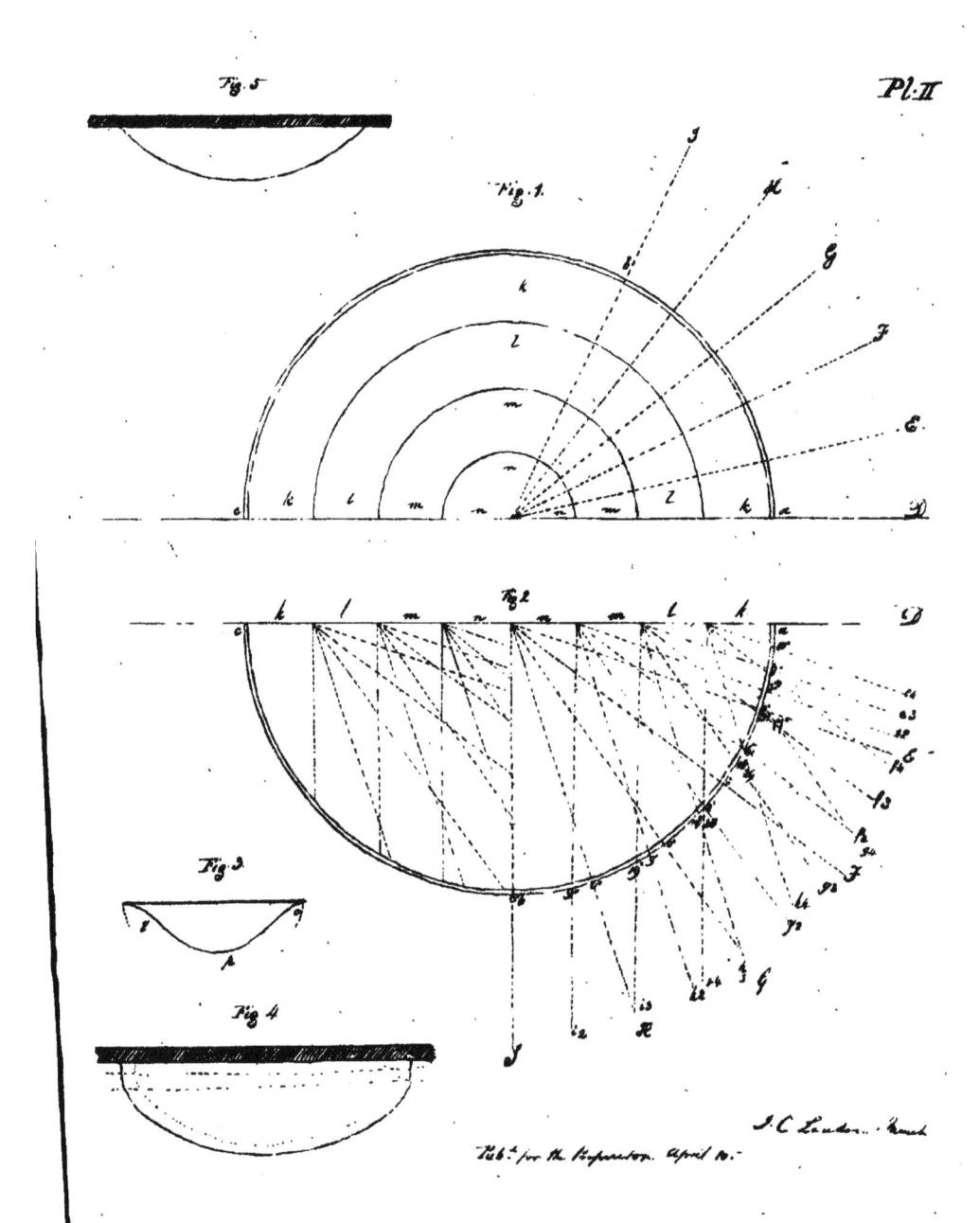

Pl: III.

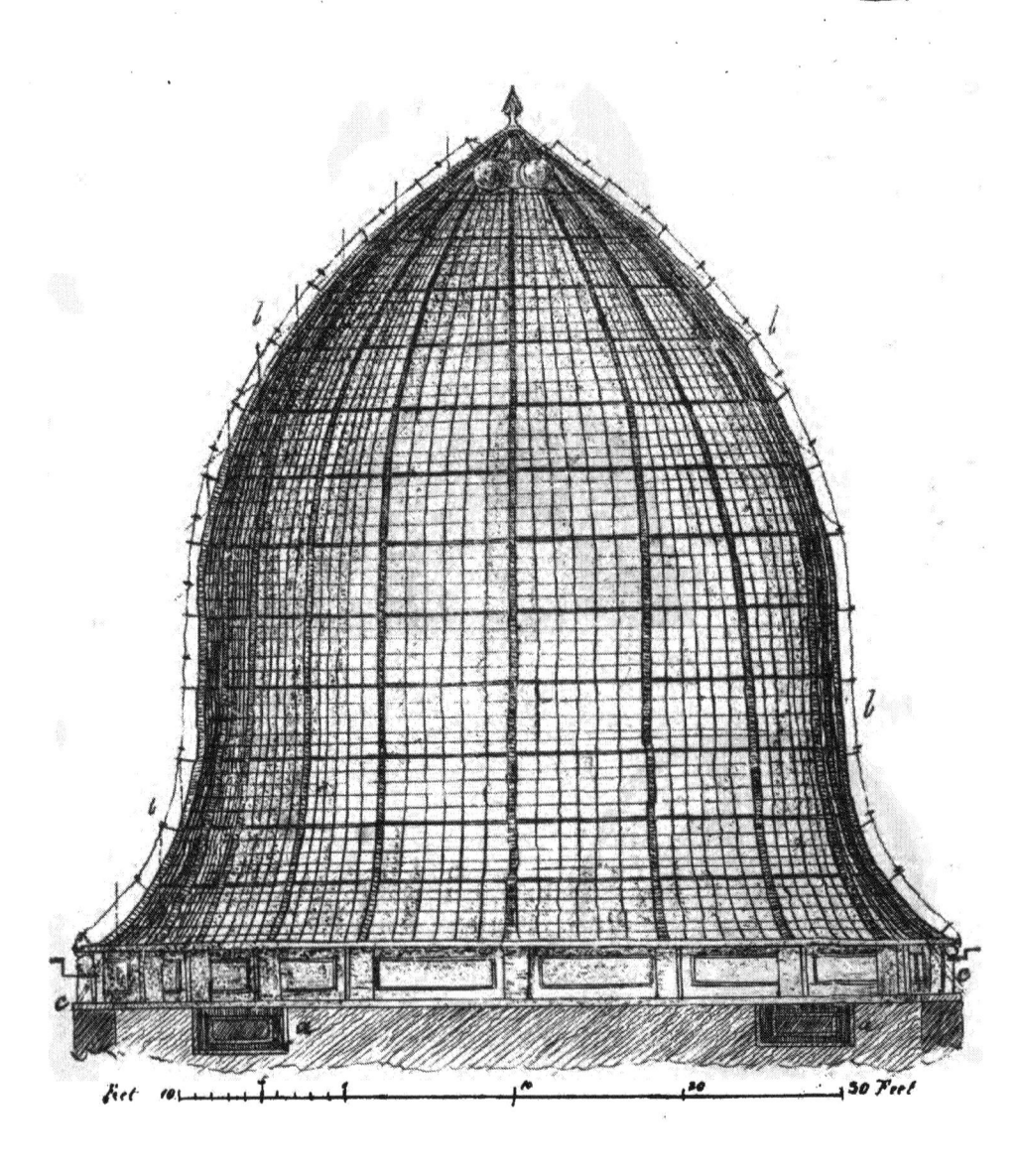

Pl. IV.

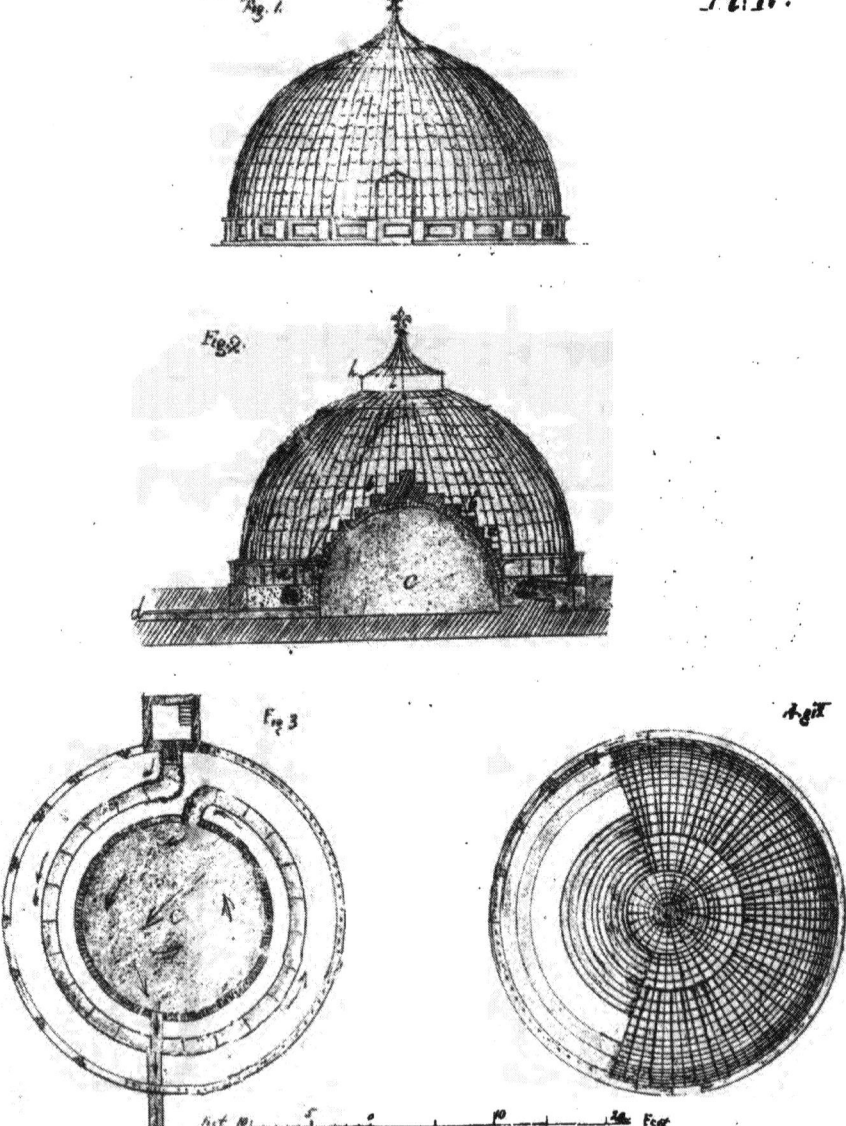

Fig. 1.

Fig. 2.

Fig. 3.

Fig. 4.

Pl. IV.

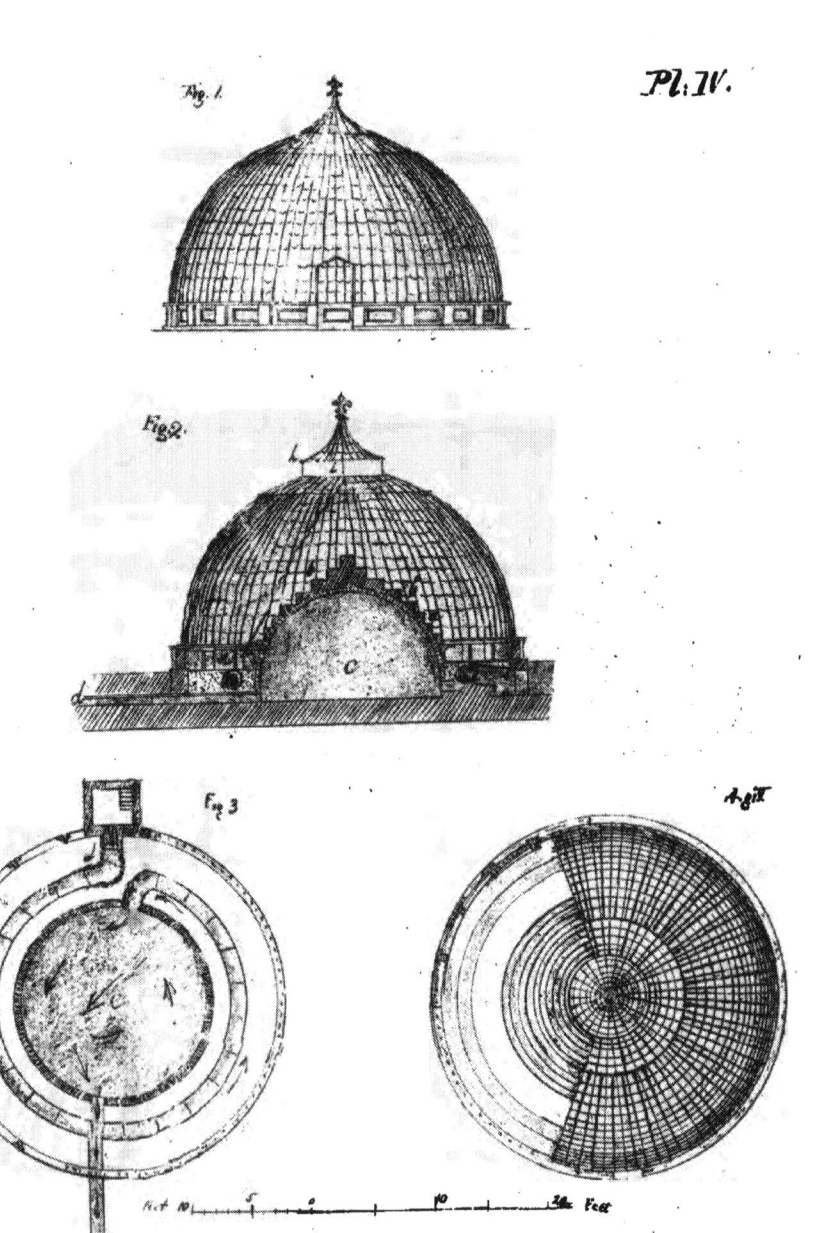

Fig. 1.

Fig. 2.

Fig. 3.

Fig. 4.

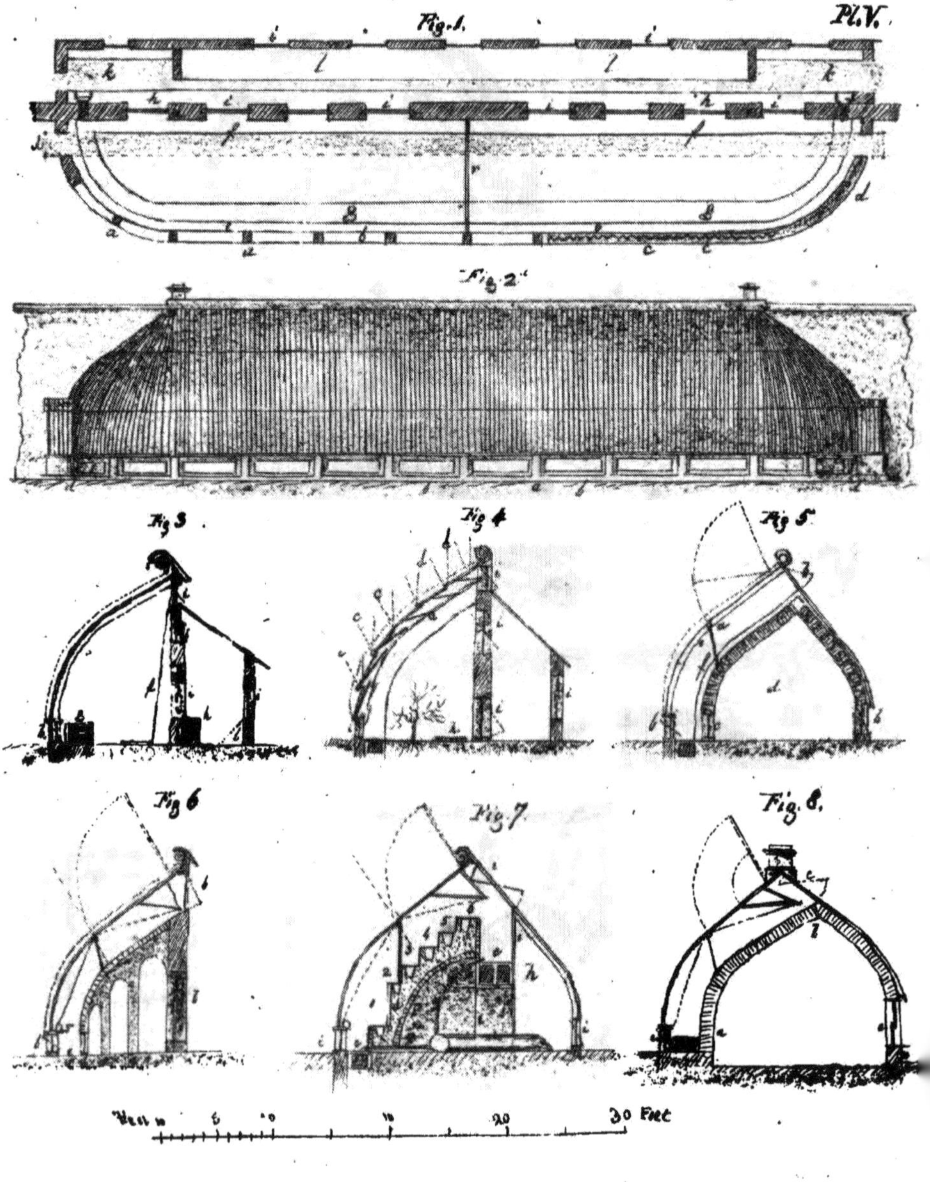

Pl. V.
Fig. 1.
Fig. 2
Fig. 3
Fig. 4
Fig. 5
Fig. 6
Fig. 7
Fig. 8.
20
30 Feet

Pl. VI.

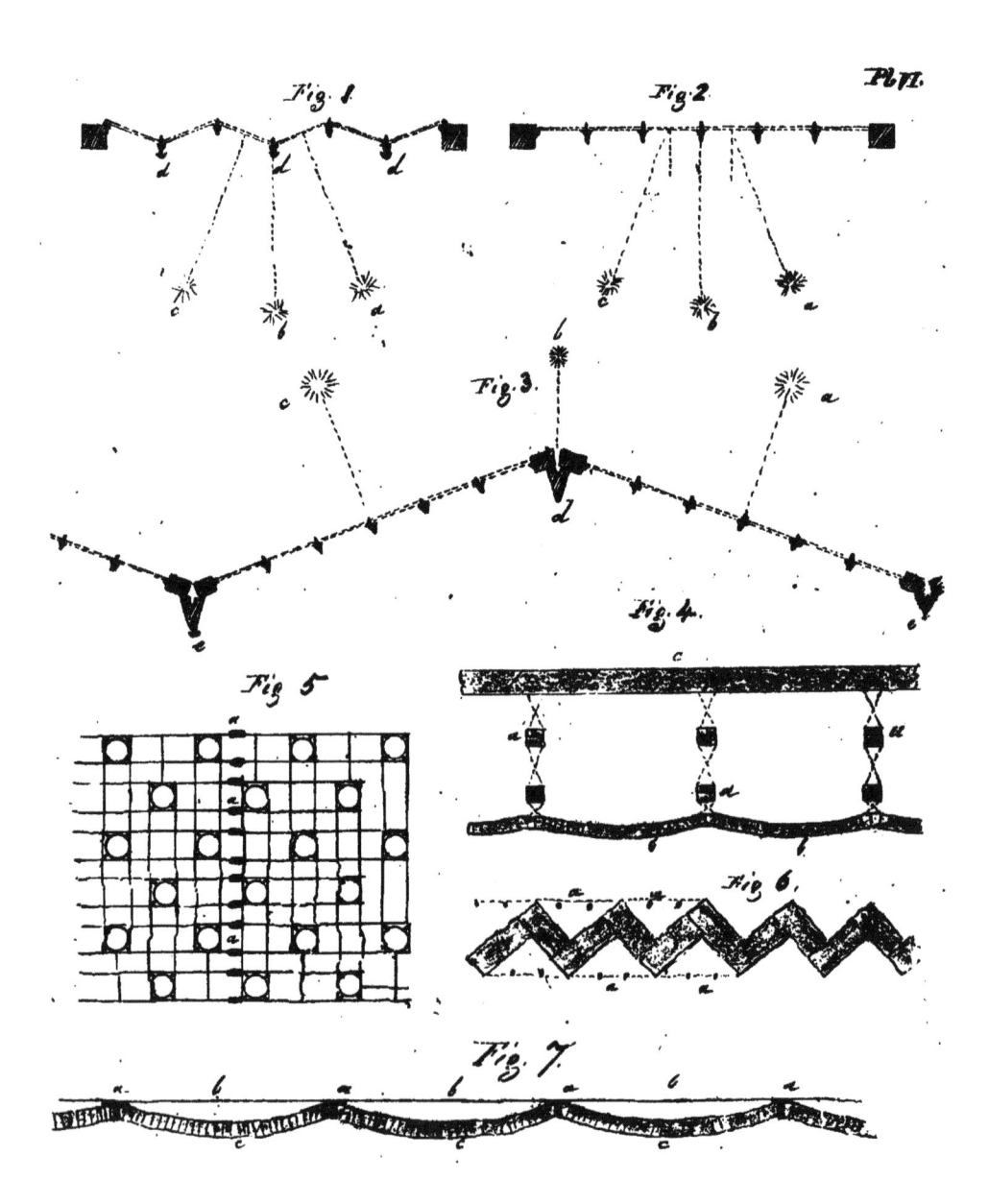

Pl. VII. Fig. 1.

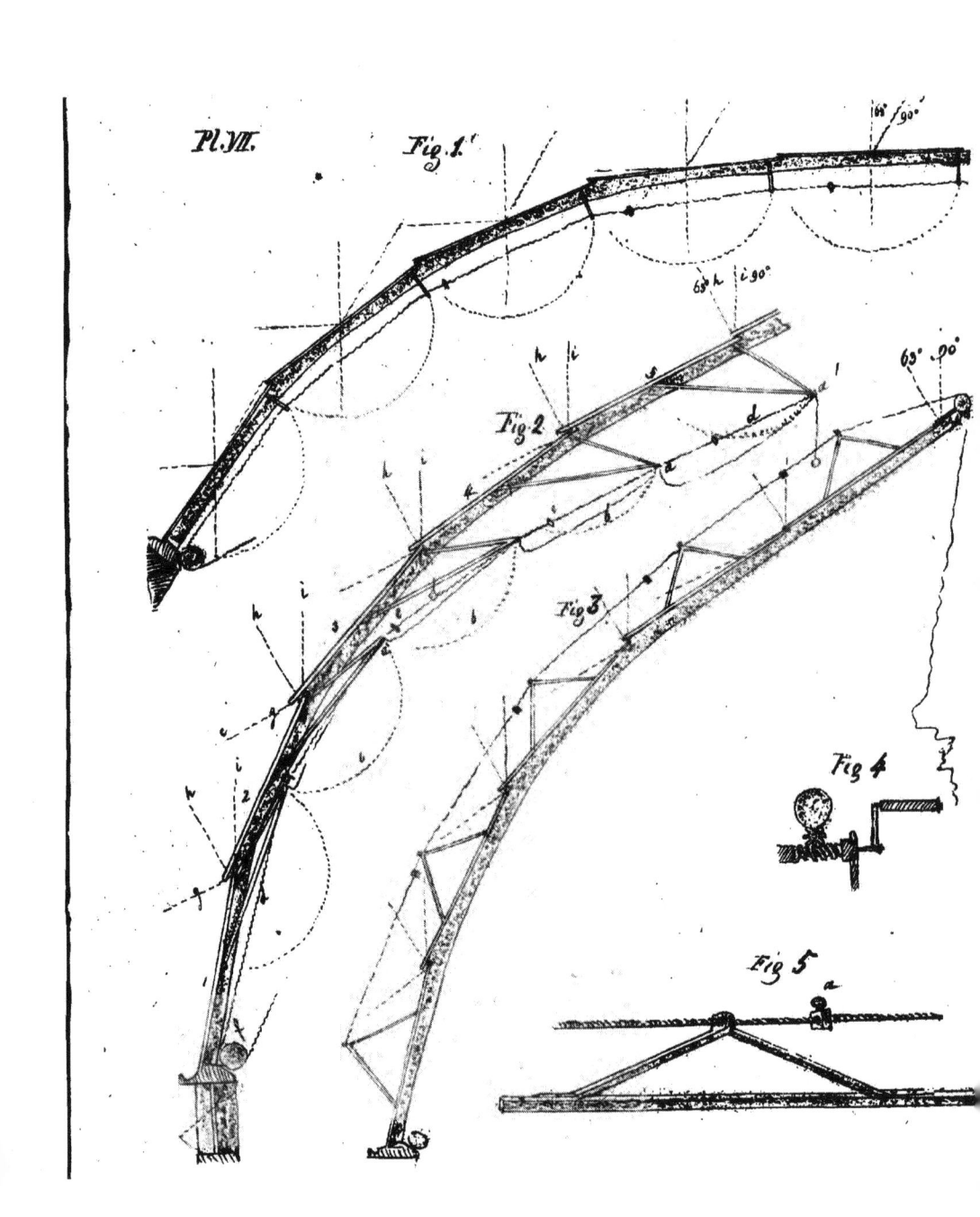

Fig. 2.

Fig. 3.

Fig. 4.

Fig. 5.

Pl. VIII

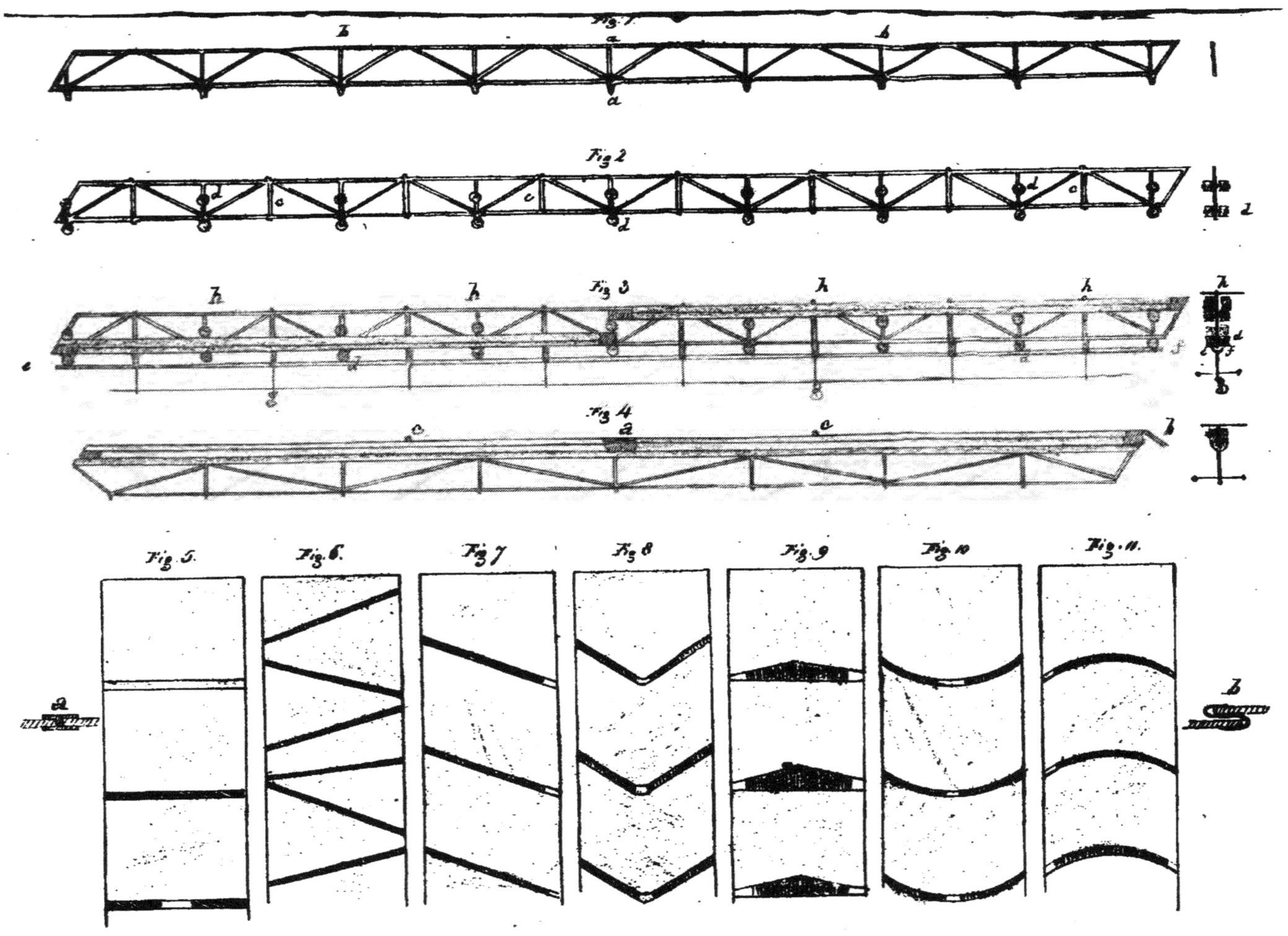

Fig. 1
Fig 2
Fig 3
Fig 4
Fig. 5.
Fig. 6.
Fig 7
Fig 8
Fig. 9
Fig. 10
Fig. 11.

Pl. X.

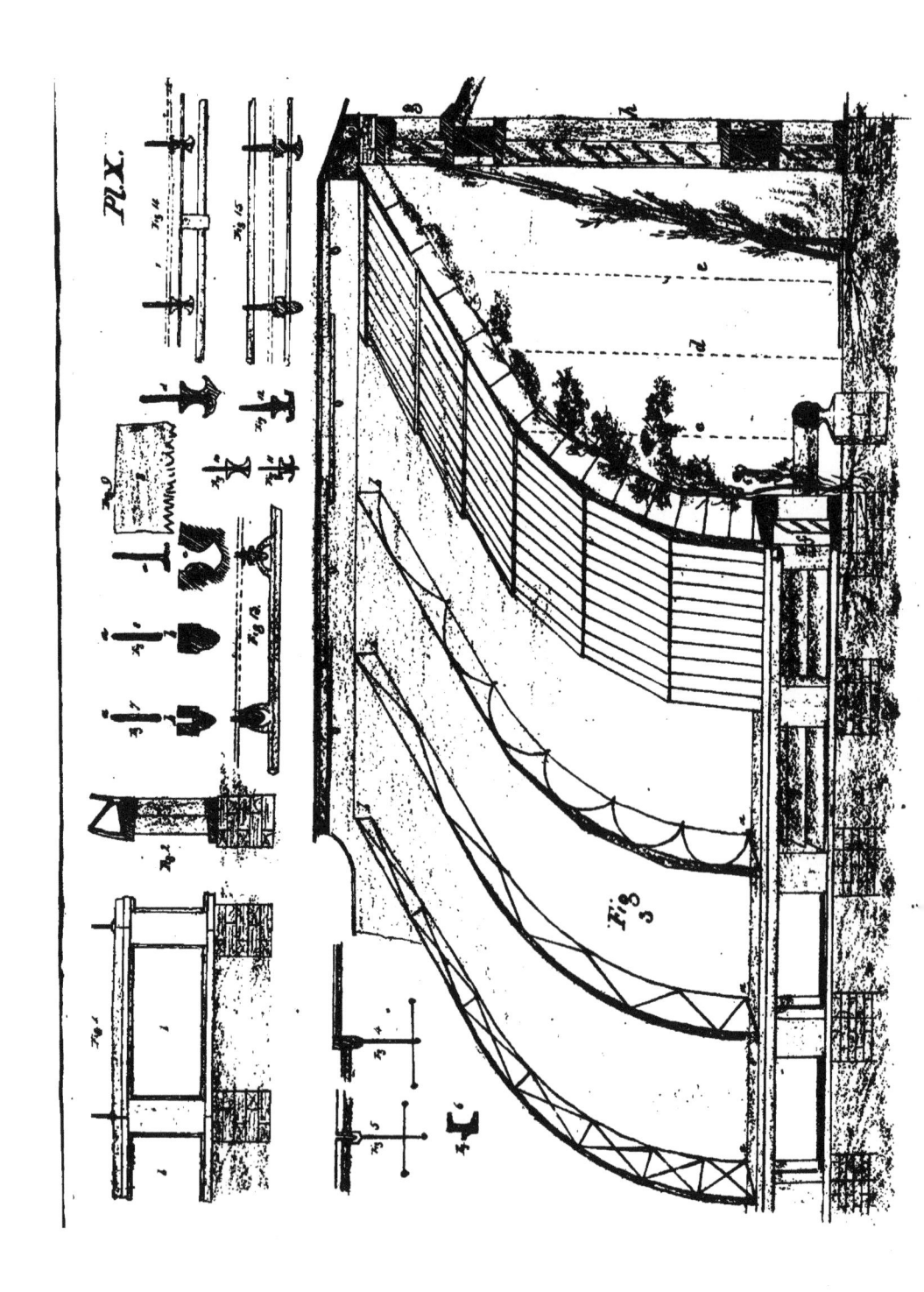

A

Catalogue

OF

MODERN BOOKS

ON

ARCHITECTURE,

THEORETICAL, PRACTICAL, AND ORNAMENTAL;

CONSISTING OF

BOOKS OF PLANS AND ELEVATIONS FOR COTTAGES, FARM-HOUSES, MANSIONS, TEMPLES, BRIDGES, &c.

OF ORNAMENTS FOR INTERNAL DECORATIONS, FOLIAGE FOR CARVERS, &c.

ON PERSPECTIVE; ALSO

PRACTICAL BOOKS FOR CARPENTERS, BRICKLAYERS, AND WORKMEN IN GENERAL,

WHICH, WITH THE BEST ANCIENT AUTHORS, ARE CONSTANTLY ON SALE AT

J. TAYLOR'S

ARCHITECTURAL LIBRARY, No. 59, HIGH HOLBORN, LONDON.

WHERE MAY BE HAD

THE WORKS OF THE MOST CELEBRATED FRENCH ARCHITECTS AND ENGINEERS.

THE *Antiquities of Athens*; measured and delineated, by *James Stuart*, F. R. S. and F. S. A. and *Nicholas Revett*, Painters and Architects, in three large Volumes Folio, Price 17*l*. 17*s*. in boards. The third Volume may be had separate to complete Sets, Price 6*l*. 13*s*. in boards—*This Work contains 281 Plates, engraved by the best Artists, of Views, Architecture, Plans, &c. with Letter-press, Historical and Descriptive, illustrating by a Research of many Years' Labour and great Expense, the purest Examples of Grecian Architecture, many of which no longer exist, and the Traces of them can be found only in this Work.*

Contents of the Work.

Doric Portico at Athens, Ionic Temple on the Ilissus, Octagon Tower of Andronicus Cyrrestes, Lanthorn of Demosthenes, Stoa, or Portico at Athens: And a large View of the Acropolis. Temple of Minerva, Temple of Erectheus, Theatre of Bacchus, Choragic Monument of Thrasyllus, &c. Propylea: And a large View, and a Plan of the Acropolis. Temple of Theseus, Temple of Jupiter, Arch of Theseus, Aquæduct of Hadrian, Monument of Philopappus, Temple of Corinth, Bridge of the Ilissus, Odeum of Regilla, Ruins at Salonica, Antiquities on the Island of Delos, &c.—Also a large Map of Greece—Map of Attica—Plan of Athens, &c.

The Fourth Vol. which is just Published, contains all the remaining Sculpture of the Temple of Minerva at Athens, with sundry Fragments found in the Greek Islands: also the entire Details of the Antiquities at Pola, in Istria, from the Drawings left by *Mr. Stuart*. Engraved 103 Plates, imperial folio, 7*l*. 7s. Boards.

An Essay on the Doric Order of Architecture, containing an historical View of its Rise and Progress among the Ancients, with a Critical Investigation of its Principles of Composition and Adaptation to Modern Use, illustrated by Figures from the principal Antique Examples, drawn to one Scale, on 7 Plates, by *E. Aikin*, Architect, large Folio, 1*l*. 5*s*. boards.

The Ancient Buildings of Rome, accurately measured and delineated, by *Antony Desgodetz*, with Explanations in French and English; the Text translated, and the Plates engraved, by the late *Mr. George Marshall*, Architect, 2 vols. imperial folio, with 137 Plates, Price 5*l*. 15*s*. 6d. sewed; or 6*l*. 16s. 6d. half bound.

Plans, Elevations, Sections and Views of the Church of *Batalha*, in the Province of Estremadura, in Portugal, with an History and Description, by Father Luis de Sousa, with Remarks, to which is prefixed an Introductory Discourse upon the Principles of Gothic Architecture, by *James Murphy*, Architect. Illustrated with 27 elegant Plates, printed on Imperial Folio, and hot-pressed, Price 4*l*. 14s. 6d. half-bound.

Specimens of Gothic Architecture, consisting of Doors, Windows, Buttresses, Pinnacles, &c. with the Measurements; selected from Ancient Buildings at Oxford, &c. Drawn and etched by F. Mackenzie and A. Pugin. On 61 Plates, Quarto, Price 2*l*. 2s. in Boards, on Demy; and on Imperial Paper 3*l*. 3s. Boards; to range with Britton's Architectural Antiquities and Cathedrals.

Specimens of Gothic Architecture, selected from the Parish Church of Lavenham, in Suffolk, on 40 Plates quarto. Price 18s. boards, on large Paper, 1*l*. 5s.

Dickinson's Architectural Antiquities of Southwell, &c. Two Parts, Quarto, with 23 elegant Plates, 1*l*. 1s. Boards.

Views of the Collegiate Chapel of *St. George*, at Windsor, on 9 very large Plates, in Aquatinta, by *F. Nash*, Price 4*l*. 4s.

Gothic Ornaments of the Cathedral Church of York, by *J. Halfpenny*, 105 Plates, large Quarto.

Fragmenta Vetusta, or the Ancient Buildings of York, by *J. Halfpenny*, 34 Plates, large Quarto, 3*l*. 3s.

The

[2]

The Rudiments of Ancient Architecture, containing an Historical Account of the Five Orders, with their Proportions, and Examples of each from Antiques: Also, Extracts from *Vitruvius*, *Pliny*, &c. relative to the Buildings of the Antients. Calculated for the Use of those who wish to attain a summary Knowledge of the Science of Architecture; with a Dictionary of Terms: illustrated with 11 Plates. The Fourth Edition, Boards, 8s.

Essays on Gothic Architecture, by the Rev. T. Warton, Rev. J. Bentham, Capt. Grose, and Rev. J. Milner. Illustrated with 12 Plates of Ornaments, &c. selected from Ancient Buildings; calculated to exhibit the various Styles of different Periods. The third Edition, with a List of the Cathedrals of England and their Dimensions. Octavo. 10s. 6d. Boards.

An Historical Survey of the Ecclesiastical Antiquities of France, with a View to illustrate the Rise and Progress of Gothic Architecture in Europe. By the late Rev. G. D. *Whittington*, of Cambridge. Elegantly printed in Royal 8vo. With a Frontispiece of the Façade of the Cathedral Church at Rheimes. 12s. Boards.

A Treatise on the *Ecclesiastical Architecture* of England, during the middle Ages, with 10 illustrative Copper Plates, by the Rev. *J. Milner*, D. D. F. S. A. Royal Octavo. 15s. Boards.

Observations on *English Architecture*, Military, Ecclesiastical, and Civil, compared with similar Buildings on the Continent; including a critical Itinerary of *Oxford* and *Cambridge*: also Historical Notices of Stained Glass, Ornamental Gardening, &c. with Chronological Tables, and Dimensions of Cathedrals and Conventual Churches, by the Rev. *James Dallaway*, M. B. F. S. A. Royal Octavo. 12s. Boards.

An History of the Origin and Establishment of *Gothic Architecture*; comprehending also an Account from his own Writings of *Cæsar Cæsarianus*, the first professed Commentator on Vitruvius, and of his Translation of that Author; an Investigation of the Principles and Proportion of that Style of Architecture called the Gothic; and an Inquiry into the Mode of Painting upon and Staining Glass, as practised in the Ecclesiastical Structures of the middle Ages. By *John Sidney Hawkins*, F. A. S. Royal Octavo, illustrated with Eleven Plates, Price 18s. in Boards.

An Essay on the Origin, History and Principles of Gothic Architecture, by Sir *James Hall*, Bart. large Quarto, handsomely printed, with 60 Plates elegantly engraved, of select Examples, 5l. 5s. in Boards.

The Builder's Price Book; containing a correct List of the Prices allowed by the most eminent Surveyors in *London* to the several Artificers concerned in Building; including the *Journeymen's Prices*. A new Edition, corrected; by an Experienced Surveyor. Sewed, 3s. 6d.

The *New Vitruvius Britannicus*, consisting of Plans and Elevations of modern Buildings, public and private, erected in Great Britain by the most celebrated *Architects*, engraved on 142 Plates, from original Drawings. By G. *Richardson*, Architect. Two Vols. Imperial Folio, half bound, 12l. 12s.

Sketches for *Cottages*, *Villas*, &c. with their Plans and appropriate Scenery, by *John Soane*; to which is added six Designs for *improving and embellishing Grounds*, with Explanations, by an *Amateur*, on 54 Plates, elegantly engraved in Aquatinta. Folio. 2l. 12s. 6d. half bound.

Plans, Elevations, and Sections of Buildings, executed in the Counties of Norfolk, Suffolk, Yorkshire, Wiltshire, Warwickshire, Staffordshire, Somersetshire, &c. by *John Soane*, Architect, on 47 Folio Plates, 2l. 12s. 6d.

Plans, Elevations, and *Sections*, of Noblemen's and Gentlemen's Houses, Stabling, Bridges public and private, Temples, and other Garden Building, executed in the Counties of Derby, Durham, Middlesex, Northumberland, Nottingham, York, Essex, Wilts, Hertford, Suffolk, Salop, and Surrey; by *James Paine*, Architect. Two Vols. with 176 very large Folio Plates, 8l. 8s. half bound.

The Designs of *Inigo Jones*, consisting of Plans and Elevations for Public and Private Buildings; including the Detail of the intended Palace at Whitehall; published by *W. Kent*, with some additional Designs. 2 Vols. Imperial Folio.

Plans, Elevations, and Sections, of *Hot-Houses*, *Green-Houses*, an *Aquarium*, *Conservatories*, &c. recently built in different Parts of England for various Noblemen and Gentlemen, by G. *Tod*, Surveyor and Hot-House Builder; including a Hot-House and a Green-House in her Majesty's Gardens at Frogmore, on 27 Plates, elegantly coloured, with proper Descriptions. Folio, 2l. 12s. 6d. in Boards.

Designs for Villas and other Rural Buildings, by *Edmund Aikin*, Architect; with Plans and Explanations. Together with an Introductory Essay, containing Remarks on the prevailing Defects of Modern Architecture, and an Investigation of the Style best adapted to the Dwellings of the present Times; engraved on 31 Plates large Quarto, Price 1l. 11s. 6d. in Boards.

A Series of Designs for Villas and Country Houses. Adapted with Economy to the Comforts and to the Elegancies of Modern Life; with Plans and Explanations to each. To which is prefixed, an Essay on Modern Architectural Taste. By C. A. *Busby*, *Architect*. Engraved in Aqua-tinta, on 24 Plates, large Quarto, in Boards, 1l. 5s.

Architectural Designs, for Rustic Cottages, Picturesque Dwellings, Villas, &c. with appropriate Scenery, Plans and Descriptions; to which are prefixed some critical Observations on their Style and Character; and also of Castles, Abbies, and ancient English Houses.— Concluding with Practical Remarks on Building, and the Causes of the *Dry Rot*. By *W. F. Pocock*, Architect. Elegantly engraved on 33 Plates, Royal Quarto, Price 1l. 11s. 6d. in Boards.

Designs for Lodges, and Entrances to Parks, Paddocks, and Pleasure Grounds, in the Gothic, Cottage, and Fancy Styles, with characteristic Scenery and Descriptions in Letter-press, by *T. D. W. Dearn*, elegantly engraved on 20 Plates, large Quarto, 1l. 11s. 6d. Boards.

Sketches in Architecture, consisting of original Designs for Cottages and Rural Dwellings, suitable to Persons of moderate Fortune, and for convenient Retirement; with Plans and appropriate Scenery to each; also some general Observations. By *T. D. W. Dearn*, Architect to his Royal Highness the Duke of Clarence. Elegantly engraved on 20 Plates, large Quarto, Price 1l. 7s. in Boards.

Plans and Views of Buildings executed in *England* and *Scotland* in the Castellated and other Styles. By *R. Lugar*, Architect, on 32 Plates Royal Quarto with descriptive Letter-press, Price 2l. 2s. in boards.

Architectural Sketches for Cottages, Rural Dwellings, and Villas: with Plans, suitable to Persons of genteel Life and moderate Fortune; proper for Picturesque Buildings, by *R. Lugar*, Architect and Land Surveyor; elegantly engraved in Aquatinta, on 38 Plates, Boards, 1l. 11s. 6d.

The Country Gentleman's Architect, containing a Variety of Designs for Farm Houses and Farm Yards of Different Magnitudes, arranged on the most approved Principles for Arable, Grazing, Feeding and Dairy Farms, with Plans and Sections, shewing at large the Construction of Cottages, Barns, Stables, Feeding Houses, Dairies, Brewhouse, &c. with Plans for Stables and Dog-kennels, and some Designs for Labourers' Cottages and small Villas. The whole adapted to the Use of Country Gentlemen about to build or to alter. Engraved on 21 Plates, with some General Observations, and full Explanations to each. By *R. Lugar*, Quarto, 1l. 5s. in Boards.

Designs for *Small Picturesque Cottages, Hunting Boxes, Park Entrances*, &c. by E. *Gyfford*, Architect. Part I. Engraved in Aquatinta, on 20 Plates, Quarto, 1l. 1s. Boards.

Designs

Designs for *Elegant Cottages*, and small Villas, calculated for the Comfort and Convenience of Persons of moderate and of ample Fortune, carefully studied and thrown into Perspective, with General Estimates, by *E. Gyfford*, Architect. Part II. Engraved in Aquatinta on 26 Plates, Quarto 1l. 11s. 6d. boards.

Hints for Dwellings, consisting of Original Designs for Cottages, Farm-houses, Villas, &c. plain and ornamental; with Plans to each, in which strict Attention is paid to unite Convenience and Elegance with Economy. Including some Designs for Townhouses. By *D. Laing*, Architect, and Surveyor. Elegantly engraved on 34 Plates in Aquatinta, with appropriate Scenery. Quarto, 1l. 5s. in boards.

Sketches for Country Houses, Villas, and Rural Dwellings; calculated for Persons of moderate Income, and for comfortable Retirement. Also some Designs for Cottages, which may be constructed of the simplest Materials; with Plans and general Estimates. By *John Plaw*. Elegantly engraved in Aquatinta on 42 Plates, Quarto, 1l. 11s. 6d. in Boards.

Ferme Ornée, or *Rural Improvements*, a Series of Domestic and Ornamental Designs, suited to Parks, Plantations, Rides, Walks, Rivers, Farms, &c. consisting of Fences, Paddock House, a Bath, Dog-kennels, Pavilions, Farm-yards, Fishing-houses, Sporting-Boxes, Shooting-lodges, Single and Double Cottages, &c. calculated for Landscape and Picturesque Effects. By *John Plaw*, Architect. Engraved in Aquatinta on 38 Plates, with appropriate Scenery. Plans, and Explanations. Quarto. In Boards, 1l. 11s. 6d.

Rural Architecture, or Designs from the Simple Cottage to the decorated Villa, including some which have been executed. By *John Plaw*. On 62 Plates, with Scenery, in Aquatinta. Half Bound, 2l. 2s.

An Essay on British Cottage Architecture, exemplified by fourteen Designs, with their Plans, &c. on 23 Plates, designed and executed by *James Malton*. The Second Edition, with two additional Plates, large Quarto, Boards, 1l. 11s. 6d.

A Collection of *Architectural Designs*, for Villas, Casinos, Mansions, Lodges, and Cottages, from original Drawings, by *James Randall*, Architect, engraved in Aquatinta, on 34 Plates, large Folio, 3l. 13s. 6d.

The Architect and Builder's Miscellany, or Pocket Library; containing original Picturesque Designs in Architecture, for Cottages, Farm, Country, and Town Houses, Public Buildings, Temples, Green-Houses, Bridges, Lodges and Gates for Entrances to Parks and Pleasure Grounds, Stables, Monumental Tombs, Garden Seats, &c. By *Charles Middleton*, Architect. On 60 Plates, coloured. Octavo. 1l. 1s. bound.

Crunden's Convenient and Ornamental Architecture; consisting of Original Designs for Plans, Elevations and Sections, beginning with the Farm-house, and regularly ascending to the most grand and magnificent Villa; calculated both for Town and Country, with Explanation in Letter-press, and exact Scales. Engraved on 70 Copper-plates, 16s. Boards.

A Series of Plans, for Cottages or Habitations for the Labourer, either in Husbandry or the Mechanic Arts, adapted as well to Towns as to the Country. To which is added, an Introduction, containing many useful Observations on this Class of building, tending to the Comfort of the Poor, and Advantage of the Builder; with Calculations of Expenses. By the late *Mr. J. Wood*, of Bath, Architect. A new Edition, corrected to the present Time, with 30 Plates, large 4to. 1l. 1s.

The Country Gentleman's Architect, in a great Variety of New Designs for Cottages, Farm-houses, Country-houses, Villas, Lodges for Park or Garden Entrances, and ornamental wooden Gates, with Plans of the Offices belonging to each Design; distributed with a strict Attention to Convenience, Elegance and Economy. On 32 Quarto Plates. By *J. Miller*, Architect. Sewed, 10s. 6d.

Essays of the London Architectural Society. Octavo, 4 Plates. 7s. Boards. Also the Second Part, 4 Plates, 8s. 6d.

Aikin's Essay on the Doric Order, 7 Plates, large Folio. 1l. 5s. Boards.

Vasi's View of Rome, on 12 Sheets, 3l. 13s. 6d.

Vitruvius Britannicus, 5 Vols.

Chambers's (Sir William) Treatise on Civil Architecture.

Chambers's Buildings and Views of Kew Gardens. Half bound, 2l. 10s.

Chambers's Designs for Chinese Buildings, &c. 1l. 11s. 6d.

Chambers's Dissertation on Oriental Gardening, 4to. 9s.

Inigo Jones's Designs, by Kent, 2 vols. folio.

Gwilt on Arches, 8vo. 4 Plates. 6s.

Ware on Arches, and their abutment Piers, octavo, 19 Plates. 18s.

Ware's Remarks on Theatres, octavo, 3 Plates. 7s.

Atwood on Arches, quarto, Two Parts. Plates. 18s.

Malton (James) Perspective, Quarto, 1l. 1s.

Wood's Lectures on Perspective, with an Apparatus. 1l. 16s.

Paine's Plans, Elevations, &c. of Noblemen's Seats, &c. folio, 2 vols. Half bound, 8l. 8s.

The Architectural Antiquities of Athens, by Stuart, 4 vols. of Rome, Balbec, Palmyra, Pœstum, Ionia, de la Grece, par *Le Roy*, &c. &c.

Wilkins' Antiquities of Magna Græcia, &c. Folio, 10l. 10s.

Wilkins' Translation of Vitruvius, Quarto.

Newton's Translation of Vitruvius, 2 vols. folio.

Murphy's Arabian Antiquities of Spain, 100 Plates, large folio, 4l.

Nicholson's Principles of Architecture, 3 vols. 8vo. 3l. 3s. boards.

A Treatise on Theatres, including some Experiments on Sound, by G. *Saunders*, Architect, with Plates, 4to. boards, 16s.

Smeaton's Description of the Edystone Lighthouse, Plates, folio. 6l. 6s.

Reports, by *J. Smeaton*, Civil Engineer, 3 vols. 4to. 7l. 7s. Boards.

Smeaton's Miscellaneous Papers, 4to. 1l. 11s. 6d. Boards.

Gray's Experienced Millwright. Folio, 44 Plates. 2l. 2s.

Imison's Elements of Science and Art. 2 Vols. 1l. 5s.

Buchanan's Practical Essays on Mill-Work. 2 Vol. 19s. boards.

Gregory's Treatise on Mechanics, 3 Vols. 2l. 2s.

Hutton's Course of Mathematics. 3 Vols. 1l. 11s. 6d.

Papworth on the Dry Rot, 3s.

Randall on the Dry Rot, 3s.

Perronet sur les Ponts, 2 Tom.

Belidor Science des Ingenieurs, 4to. New Edition, with new Plates, &c.

Belidor,

[4]

Belidor, D'Architecture Hydraulique, 4 Tom. Quarto.
Nouvelle Arch. Hydraulique, par Prony, 2 Tom.
Piranesi's Works, complete, 23 Vols. large Folio.
Rafael's Ornaments of the Vatican, 3 Parts, Folio.
Dictionnaire d'Architecture, Civile, Militaire et Navale, par Roland, 3 Tom. Quarto, with 100 Plates.
Plans, Coupes, et Elevations des plus belles Maisons et des Hotels, à Paris, et dans les Environs, avec des Ornemens. Folio, 120 Plates.
Durand Leçons d'Architecture, 2 Tom. 4to.
Durand Recueil et Parallele des Edifices Anciens et Modernes. 92 very large folio Plates.
Plans, Coupes et Elevations de diverses Productions de l'Art de la Charpente, par Krafft. 201 Plates, large Folio.
Ornamenti di Albertoli, 3 Parts, Folio.
Museo Pio Clementino, 7 Tom.
Museo Chiaramonti.
Wiebeking on Bridges, Draining, &c. In German. 3 Vols. 4to. and a large Atlas.
Wiebeking des Ponts à Arches de Charpente, 4to. with a large Atlas of 20 plates.
Ornemens de le Pautre. 3 Vols. Folio.
Bourse de Paris, par Brouginard.
Œvores de Weyrotter.
Voyage de la Grece, par Choiseuil Gouffiere. 2 Vols.
Antiquité de Poestum, par Delagardette. Folio.
Ornemens de Cauvet. Folio.
Voyage Pittoresque de l'Istria, par Casas. Folio.
Voyage Pittoresque de la Suisse. 4 Vols. Folio.
Voyage Pittoresque de Naple et Sicile. 5 Vols. Folio.
Voyage Pittoresque des Isles de Sicile, de Malte et de Lipari, par Houel. 4 Vols. Folio.
Suite de Paysage, de Bourgin. Folio.
Cabinet de Choiseuil.
Cabinet de Poulain. Proofs.
Coupe de Pierre, par Gardelle.
Canaux Navigables, de Lalande, Folio.
Canal du Midi, par Andreossi. 2 Vols. 4to.
Encyclopedie de l'Ingenieur, par Delaitre. 3 Vols. 8vo. and Atlas of Plates.
Pousse des Terres, par Maignes, 4to.
Traité de l'Art de Batir, par Rondelet. 5 Vols. 4to. Plates.

Programme du Course de Construction, par Sganzin, 4to.
Decorations par Percier et Fontains, Folio.
Palais et Maisons de Rome, par Percier, Folio.
Italia avant il Dominio di Romani, par Micali. 4 Vols. 8vo. and Atlas.
Manuel du Tourneur. 2 Vols. 4to. Plates.
Dictionnaire des Graveurs. 2 Vols. 8vo. Plates.
Cabinet des Pierres-gravées, de Duc d'Orleans. 2 Vols.
Memoire de l'Architecture, par Patte, 4to.
Coupe de Pierres, de Freziere, 3 Vols. 4to.
Description du Pont à Moulins, par Régemorte, Folio.
Boulet Machines de Theatre.
Scrittori dell'acqua. 8 Vols. 4to.
Paris et ses Monumens, par Baltard. Folio.
Musée des Monumens Francais, par Lenoir. 6 Vol. 8vo.
Annales du Musée, par Landon.
Bossut Traité d'Hydrodynamique. 2 Vols. 8vo.
Bossut et Viallet sur la Construction des Digues.
Bremontier sur le Mouvement des Ondes.
Decessart Travaux Hydrauliques. 2 Vols. 4to.
Ducrest D'Hydraufonie.
Les Fontaines de Paris, par Duval.
Gauthey de la Construction des Ponts. 2 Vols. 4to.
Lesage divers Memoires des Ponts et Chaussées. 2 Vols. 4to.
Navier, Projet d'une Gare à Choisy.
Sakolniki Hydrodynamique.
Berard Statique des Voûtes.
Brunet, dimension des Fers qui doivent former la coupole de la Halle aux Grains.
Pyre, Restauration du Pantheon.
Clocher Plans de Maisons, &c. D'Italie. Folio.
Costume Hollandoise. Plates, coloured.
Voyage en Holland. 5 Vols. 8vo. Plates.
Statistique d'Amsterdam.
Guide du Voyageur en Hollande.
New Principles of Linear Perspective, or the Art of Designing on a Plane, the representation of all Sorts of Objects in a more general and simple Method than has been hitherto done. Illustrated by 13 Quarto Plates. By Dr. Brook Taylor, LL.D. and R.SS. The Fourth Edition, 8vo. 14s. in boards.
Dr. Brook Taylor's Method of Perspective made easy both in Theory and Practice; in two Books: being an Attempt to make the Art of Perspective easy and familiar, to adapt it entirely to the Arts of Design,

[5]

Design, and to make it an entertaining Study to any Gentleman who shall choose so Polite an Amusement. By *Joshua Kirby*. Illustrated with 35 Copper-plates. The Third Edition, with several Additions and Improvements. Elegantly printed on Imperial Paper. Half Bound, 2l. 12s. 6d.

The Perspective of Architecture, a Work entirely new; deduced from the Principles of Dr. Brook Taylor and performed by two Rules of universal Application. Illustrated with 73 Plates. Begun by Command of his present Majesty when Prince of Wales. By *Joshua Kirby*. Elegantly printed on Imperial Paper. 3l. 3s. half bound.

The Description and Use of a new Instrument called the Architectonic Sector, by which any Part of Architecture may be drawn with Facility and Exactness. By *Joshua Kirby*. Illustrated with 25 Plates; elegantly printed on imperial Paper. Half bound, 1l. 16s.
The two Frontispieces, by Hogarth, to Kirby's Perspective, may be had separate, each 5s.

Modern Finishings for Rooms, a Series of Designs for Vestibules, Halls, Stair Cases, Dressing Rooms, Boudoirs, Libraries, and Drawing Rooms, with their Doors, Chimney Pieces, and other finishings to a large Scale, and the several Mouldings and Cornices at full Size, showing their Construction and relative Proportions: to which are added some Designs for Villas and Porticos, with the Rules for drawing the Columns, &c. at large. The whole adapted for the Use and Direction of every Person engaged in the practical Parts of Building, by *W. F. Pocock*, Architect, on 86 Plates, quarto, 2l. 2s. bound.

The Student's Instructor in drawing and working the Five Orders of Architecture; fully explaining the best Methods of striking regular and quirked Mouldings, for diminishing and glueing of Columns and Capitals, for finding the true Diameter of an Order to any given Height, for striking the Ionic Volute circular and elliptical, with finished Examples, on a large Scale, of the Orders, their Planceers, &c. and some Designs for Door Cases, by *Peter Nicholson*, engraved on 41 Plates octavo. 10s. 6d. bound. A new Edition corrected and much enlarged.

The Carpenter's New Guide, being a complete Book of Lines for Carpentry and Joinery, treating fully on Practical Geometry, Soffits, Brick and Plaster Groins, Niches of every Description, Sky-lights, Lines for Roofs and Domes, with a great Variety of Designs for Roofs, Trussed Girders, Floors, Domes, Bridges, &c. Stair-cases and Hand-rails of various Constructions. Angle-Bars for Shop Fronts, and Raking Mouldings, with many other Things entirely new: the Whole founded on true Geometrical Principles, the Theory and Practice well explained and fully exemplified on 84 Copper-Plates; including some Observations and Calculations on the Strength of Timber, by *P. Nicholson*, 4to. 1l. 1s. the Sixth Edition corrected and enlarged.

The Carpenter and Joiner's Assistant, containing Practical Rules for making all Kinds of Joints, and various Methods of Hingeing them together; for hanging of Doors on straight or circular Plans; for fitting up Windows and Shutters to answer various Purposes, with Rules for hanging them ;for the Construction of Floors, Partitions, Soffits, Groins, Arches for Masonry: for constructing Roofs in the best Manner from a given Quantity of Timber; for placing of Bond-Timbers; with various Methods for adjusting Raking Pediments, enlarging and diminishing of Mouldings, taking Dimensions for Joinery, and for setting out Shop Fronts; with a new Scheme for constructing Stairs and Hand-rails, and for Stairs having a conical Well-hole, &c. &c. To which are added, Examples of Various Roofs executed, with the Scantlings from actual Measurements, with Rules for Mortices and Tenons, and for fixing Iron Straps, &c. Also Extracts from M. Belidor, M. du Hamel, M. de Buffon, &c. on the Strength of Timber, with practical Observations. Illustrated with 79 Plates, and copious Explanations. By *Peter Nicholson*. Quarto 1l. 1s. bound. The third Edition, revised and corrected,

The Practical House Carpenter, or Youth's Instructor: containing a great Variety of useful Designs in Carpentry and Architecture; as Centering for Groins, Niches, &c. Examples for Roofs, Sky-lights, &c. The Five Orders laid down by a New Scale. Mouldings, &c. at large, with their Enrichments. Plans, Elevations, and Sections of Houses for Town and Country, Lodges, Hot-houses, Greenhouses, Stables, &c. Design for a Church, with Plan, Elevation, and two Sections; an Altar-piece, and Pulpit. Designs for Chimney-pieces, Shop Fronts, Door Cases. Section of a Dining-room and Library. Variety of Stair Cases, with many other important Articles and useful Embellishments. To which is added, a List of Prices for Materials and Labour, Labour only, and Day Prices. The whole illustrated and made perfectly easy by 148 quarto Copper-plates, with Explanations to each. By *William Pain*. The sixth Edition, with large Additions. 18s. bound.
N. B. This is PAIN's last Work.

The Carpenter's Pocket Directory: containing the best Methods of framing Timbers of all Figures and Dimensions, with their several Parts; as Floors, Roofs in Ledgements, their Length and Backings; Trussed Roofs, Spires, and Domes, Trussing Girders, Partitions, and Bridges, with Abutments; Centering for Arches, Vaults, &c. cutting Stone Ceilings, Groins, &c. with their Moulds: Centres for drawing Gothic Arches, Ellipses, &c. With the Plan and Sections of a Barn. Engraved on 24 Plates, with Explanations. By *W. Pain*, Architect and Carpenter. Bound, 5s.

Decorations for Parks and Gardens; Designs for Gates, Garden Seats, Alcoves, Temples, Baths, Entrance Gates, Lodges, Facades, Prospect Towers, Cattle Sheds, Ruins, Bridges, Green-houses, &c. &c. Also a Hot-house, and Hot-wall, with Plans and Scales; neatly engraved on 55 Plates, octavo. 10s. 6d. sewed.

Designs in Architecture, consisting of Plans, Elevations, and Sections for Temples, Baths, Cassinos, Pavilions, Garden Seats, Obelisks, and other Buildings; for decorating Pleasure-grounds, Parks, Forests, &c. &c. by *John Soane*. Engraved on 38 Copper-plates, 8vo. Sewed, 6s.

Grotesque Architecture, or Rural Amusement; consisting of Plans, and Elevations, for Huts, Hermitages, Chinese, Gothic and Natural Grottos, Moresque Pavilions, &c. many of which may be executed with Flints, irregular Stones, rude Branches and Roots of Trees; containing 28 Designs. By *W. Wright*. Octavo. Sewed, 4s. 6d.

Ideas for Rustic Furniture, proper for Garden Chairs, Summer Houses, Hermitages, Cottages, &c. engraved on 25 Plates. Octavo. Price 4s.

Designs for Gates and Rails, suitable to Parks, Pleasure-Grounds, Balconies, &c. Also some Designs for Trellis Work. On 27 Plates. By *C. Middleton*. Octavo, 6s.

The Carpenter's Treasure: a Collection of Designs for Temples, with their Plans; Gates, Doors, Rails, and Bridges, in the Gothic Taste, with Centres at large for striking Gothic Curves and Mouldings, and some Specimens of Rails in the Chinese Taste, forming a complete System for Rural Decorations. By *N. Wallis*, Architect. 16 Plates. Octavo. Sewed, 2s. 6d.

Gothic Architecture improved, by Rules and Proportions in many grand Designs of Columns, Doors, Windows, Chimney-Pieces, Arcades, Colonnades, Porticos, Umbrellas, Temples, Pavilions, &c. with Plans, Elevations, and Profiles, geometrically exemplified. By *B. & T. Langley*. To which is added, an Historical Discourse on Gothic Architecture. On 64 Plates Quarto. Bound, 15s.

Thirty Capitals of Columns, with six Friezes, from the *Antique*. Engraved in Aquatinta by *G. Richardson*, on 18 Plates. 4to. 15s.

Designs for *Monuments*, including *Grave-stones, Compartments, Wall-pieces*, and *Tombs*. Elegantly engraved on 40 quarto Plates. Half bound, 16s.

Designs

Designs for *Chimney-Pieces*, with Mouldings and Bases at large on 27 quarto Plates, 10s. 6d.

Designs for *Shop Fronts* and *Door Cases*, on 27 Plates. 4to. 10s. 6d.

Outlines of Designs for *Shop Fronts* and *Door Cases*, with the Mouldings at large, and Enrichments to each Design. Engraved on 24 Plates. Quarto, 5s.

Langley's Builder's Jewel. Bound, 5s.

Hawney's Complete Measurer, a new Edition, much improved, 4s. 6d.

Hoppus's Timber Measurer. Tables ready cast. 4s.

Plate Glass Book. 4s.

The *Joiner and Cabinet-maker's Darling*; containing sixty different Designs for all Sorts of Frets, Friezes, &c. Sewed, 3s.

The *Carpenter's Companion*; containing 33 Designs for all Sorts of Chinese Railing and Gates. Octavo. Sewed, 2s.

The *Carpenter's Complete Guide* to the whole System of Gothic Railing; containing 32 Designs, with Scales to each. Octavo. Sewed, 2s.

A Geometrical View of the Five Orders of Columns in Architecture adjusted by aliquot Parts; whereby the meanest Capacity, by Inspection, may delineate and work an entire Order, or any Part, of any Magnitude required. On a large Sheet, 1s.

Elevation of the New Bridge at Black Friars, with the Plan of the Foundation and Superstructure. by *R. Baldwin*; 12 Inches by 48 Inches, 5s.

Plans, Elevations, and Sections of the Machines and Centering used in erecting Black Friars' Bridge; drawn and engraved by *R. Baldwin*, Clerk of the Work; on 7 large Plates, with Explanations. 10s. 6d.

Elevation of the Stone Bridge built over the Severn at *Shrewsbury*; with the Plan of the Foundation and Superstructure, elegantly engraved by *Rooker*. 1s. 6d.

A Treatise on Building in Water. By *G. Semple*. Quarto, with 63 Plates. Sewed, 16s.

Plans, Elevation and Sections of the curious Wooden Bridge at *Schaffhausen* in Switzerland, built in 1760 by *Ulric Grubenman*, and lately destroyed by the French. 19 Inches by 29. Price 12s. coloured, with a descriptive Account in Letter-Press.

Perspective View of the proposed Iron Bridge at London, of 600 Feet Span; by *Telford*. Size 4 Feet by 2 Feet, Coloured 2l. 2s.

London and Westminster Improved. Illustrated by Plans. By *John Gwynn*, Architect. Boards.

Observations on *Brick Bond*, as practised at various periods; containing an Investigation of the best Disposition of Bricks in a Wall, for procuring the greatest possible Strength; with Figures representing the different Modes of Construction. Octavo, 1s.

The *Bricklayer's Guide* to the Mensuration of all Sorts of Brick Work, according to the *London Practice*: With Observations on the Causes and Cure of Smoaky Chimnies, the Formation of Drains, and the best Construction of Ovens, to be heated with Coals. Also, a Variety of Practical and Useful Information on this important Branch of the Building Art. Illustrated by various Figures and Nine Copper Plates. By *T. W. Dearn*, Architect. Octavo, 7s. Boards.

Tables for the Purchasing of Estates, Freehold, Copyhold, or Leasehold, Annuities, &c. and for the renewing of Leases held under Cathedral Churches, Colleges, or other Corporate Bodies, for Terms or Years certain, and for Lives. Together with several useful and interesting Tables, connected with the subject. Also the Five Tables of compound Interest. By *W. Inwood*, Architect and Surveyor. In small Octavo for a Pocket Book, 7s. in Boards.

BOOKS OF ORNAMENTS, &c.

A Collection of Antique Vases, Altars, Paterns, Tripods, Candelabra, Sarcophagi, &c. from various Museums and Collections, engraved in Outline on 170 Plates, by *H. Moses*, with Historical Essays. 5l. 5s. Half Bound small Quarto, and on large fine Paper, 5l. 5s. in extra Boards.

Ornamental Designs after the Manner of the Antique. Composed for the Use of Architects, Ornamental Painters, Statuaries, Carvers, Carpet, Silk, and printed Calico Manufactures, and every Trade dependent on the Fine Arts, by *G. Smith*, with Descriptions. Quarto. Neatly engraved in Outline. Royal 4to. on 43 Plates, Price 2l. 2s. in Boards.

A Collection of Designs for Modern Embellishments suitable to Parlours, Dining and Drawing Rooms, Folding Doors, Chimney Pieces, Varandas, Frizes, &c. By *C. A. Busby, Architect*; neatly engraved on 14 Plates, 14 of which are elegantly coloured; large Quarto. Price 1l. 11s. 6d.

Designs for the Decoration of Rooms in the various Styles of modern Embellishment. With Pilasters and Frizes at large. On 20 folio Plates, Drawn and Etched by *G. Cooper*, Draftsman and Decorator. 2l. 2s.

Ornaments Displayed, on a full Size for working, proper for all Carvers, Painters, &c. containing a Variety of accurate Examples of Foliage and Frizes, elegantly engraved in the Manner of Chalks, on 33 large Folio Plates. Sewed, 15s.

Pergolesi's Ornaments in the Etruscan and Grotesque Styles, large Folio, 5l. 5s. Boards.

A New Book of Ornaments; containing a Variety of elegant Designs for modern Pannels, commonly executed in Stucco, Wood, or Painting, and used in Decorating principal Rooms. Drawn and etched by *P. Columbani*. Quarto. Sewed, 7s. 6d.

A Variety of Capitals, Frizes, and Cornices; how to increase or decrease them, still retaining the same Proportion as the Original. Likewise 12 Designs for Chimney-pieces. On 12 Plates, drawn and etched by *P. Columbani*. Folio, Sewed, 6s.

The *Principles of Drawing Ornaments* made easy, by proper Examples of Leaves for Mouldings, Capitals, Scrolls, Husks, Foliage, &c. Engraved in Imitation of Drawings, on 16 Plates, with Instructions for learning without a Master. Particularly useful to Carvers, Cabinet-makers, Stucco-workers, Painters, Smiths, and every one concerned in Ornamental Decorations. By *an Artist*. Quarto. Sewed, 4s. 6d.

Ornamental Iron Work, or Designs in the present Taste, for Fanlights, Stair-Case Railing, Window Guard Irons, Lamp-Irons, Palisadoes, and Gates. With a Scheme for adjusting Designs with Facility and Accuracy to any Slope. Engraved on 21 Plates. Quarto. Sewed, 6s.

A new Book of Ornaments, by *S. Alken*, on 6 Plates, sewed, 2s. 6d.

Law's new Book of Ornaments. Sewed, 2s.

A Book

A Book of Vases, by *T. Law*. Sewed, 1s.

A Book of Vases, by *P. Columbani*. Sewed, 2s.

A new Book of *Eighteen Vases*, Modern and Antique, 2s.

A Book of Vases from the Antique, on 12 Plates, 2s.

An interior View of *Durham Cathedral*, and a View of the elegant *Gothic Shrine* in the same. Elegantly engraved on two large Sheets. Size 19 by 22. The Pair 12s.

An exterior and interior View of *St. Giles's Church in the Fields*, engraved by Walker. Size 18 Inches by 15. The Pair 5s.

A North-west View of Greenwich Church, 2s.

An elegant engraved View of Shoreditch Church, 38 Inches by 20, 3s.

An elegant engraved View of the *Monument* at London, with the Parts geometrically; Size 21 by 33 Inches, from an Original, by Sir C. Wren, 7s. 6d.

Sir *Christopher Wren's* Plan for rebuilding the *City* of *London* after the great Fire, 1666. 1s.

West Elevation of *York Minster*, elegantly engraved from a Drawing by *James Malton*, Price 15s.

The Building Act of the 14th Geo. III. with Plates shewing the proper Thickness of Party Walls, External Walls, and Chimneys. A complete Index, List of Surveyors and their Residence, &c. In a small Pocket Size. Sewed, 3s.

N. B. The Notice and Certificate required by the above Act, may be had printed with blank Spaces for filling up, Price 2d. each, or 13 for 2s.

Experiments and Observations made with a View of improving the Art of composing and applying *Calcareous Cements*, and of preparing *Quick Lime*; with the Theory of these Arts. By *B. Higgins*, M. D.

A General History of Inland Navigation, Foreign and Domestic; containing a Complete Account of the Canals already executed in England; with Considerations on those projected: to which are added, Practical Observations. A new Edit. Octavo, 10s. 6d. Boards.

A Map of England, shewing the Lines of the Canals executed, those proposed, and the navigable Rivers, coloured. On a large Sheet, 5s.

A Treatise on the Improvement of Canal Navigation, exhibiting the numerous Advantages to be derived from *Small Canals* and Boats of two to five Feet wide, containing from two to five Tons Burthen; with a Description of the Machinery for facilitating Conveyance by Water, through the most mountainous Countries, independent of Locks and Aqueducts; including Observations on the great Importance of Water Communications; with Thoughts on, and Designs for, Aqueducts and Bridges of Iron and Wood. By *R. Fulton*, Engineer. With 17 Plates. Quarto, Boards, 18s.

Observations on the various Systems of Canal Navigation, with Inferences practical and mathematical, in which Mr. Fulton's Plan of Wheel Boats, and the Utility of subterraneous and small Canals are particularly investigated; including an Account of the Canals and inclined Planes of China, with 4 Plates. By *W. Chapman*, Civil Engineer. Quarto. 6s. sewed.

Remarkable Ruins and Romantic Prospects of North Britain, with ancient Monuments and singular Subjects of Natural History, by the *Rev. C. Cordiner*, of Banff, with 100 Plates, elegantly engraved by Mazell. 2 Vols. Quarto. 5l. 5s. Boards.

A new Collection of 100 Views in Rome and its Vicinity, neatly engraved by *Prouti*, Quarto, Price 1l. 1s.

A Treatise on Painting, by *Leonardo da Vinci*. Faithfully translated from the original Italian, and now first digested under proper Heads, By *J. F. Rigaud*, Esq. R. A. Illustrated with 23 Copper Plates and other Figures. To which is prefixed, a new Life of the Author, drawn up from authentic Materials till now inaccessible, by *J. S. Hawkins*, Esq. F. A. S. Royal Octavo, 13s. 6d. Boards.

An Enquiry into the Changes of Taste in Landscape Gardening; to which are added, some Observations on its Theory and Practice, including a Defence of the Art. By *H. Repton*, Esq. Octavo, 5s.

Hints for Picturesque Improvements in Ornamented Cottages and their Scenery; including some Observations on the Labourer and his Cottage. Illustrated by Sketches, by *E. Bartell, Jun*. large Octavo, Boards, 10s. 6d.

Cromer considered as a Watering Place, with Observations on the Picturesque Scenery in its Neighbourhood, by *E. Bartell, Jun*. with two Views and a Map. Octavo, 8s. Boards.

Specimens of Ancient Carpentry, consisting of Framed Roofs selected from various Ancient Buildings, Public and Private. Also some Specimens of Mouldings for Cornices, Doors, and Windows, by the late Mr. *James Smith*, engraved on 36 Plates, Quarto, Price 12s. sewed.

The Architectural Antiquities of Great Britain, represented and illustrated in a Series of Views, Elevations, Plans, Sections and Details, of Various Ancient English Edifices, with Historical and Descriptive Accounts of each. By *John Britton*, F. S. A. 4 Vols. Quarto, with 278 elegant engraved Plates, 21l. in Boards, and on large Paper 32l.

N. B. The parts may be had separate to complete Sets at 10s. 6d. each, large Paper 16s.

An Historical and Architectural Essay, relating to Redcliffe Church, Bristol, illustrated with 12 engravings of Plans, Views and Details, with an Account of the Monuments, and Anecdotes of eminent Persons connected with the Church. Royal Octavo, 16s. Medium Quarto, 1l. 4s. and Imperial Quarto, 1l. 11s. 6d.

N. B. The Quarto sizes will range with the Architectural Antiques.

The Cathedral Antiquities of England, or an Historical, Architectural and Graphical Illustration of the English Cathedral Churches. By *John Britton*, F. S. A. Of this work, one Part, containing 6 or 7 Plates, will be published every three Months, Price 12s. Medium Quarto, and on Imperial Quarto 1l.

N. B. Salisbury Cathedral is completed in 5 Parts.—*Norwich Cathedral* is completed in 4 Parts.—Winchester Cathedral is now publishing.

The Fine Arts of the English School, illustrated by a Series of Engravings from Paintings, Sculpture, and Architecture, by eminent English Artists, with Historical, Critical, and Biographical Letterpress, edited by *J. Britton*, F. S. A. This Volume contains 24 highly finished Engravings, Elephant Quarto, price 5l. 5s. extra Boards; on Atlas Quarto, with first Impressions, price 8l. 8s. extra Boards.

Plans, Elevation, Section, &c. &c. of the Cathedral Church of *St. Paul's*, London, with an Historical and Descriptive Account. By *E. Aikin*, Architect. On Elephant Quarto, Price 2l. 2s. and on Atlas Quarto, Price 3l. 3s. in Boards.

A

A COLLECTION of DESIGNS for Household Furniture and interior Decoration, in the most approved and elegant Taste, viz. Curtains, Draperies, Beds, Cornices, Chairs and Sofas for Parlors, Libraries, Drawing Rooms, &c. Library Fauteuils, Seats, Ottomans, Chaise Longue, Tables for Libraries, Writing, Work, Dressing, &c. Sideboards, Celerets, Book-cases, Screens, Candelabri, Chiffoniers, Commodes, Pier Tables, Wardrobes, Pedestals, Glasses, Mirrors, Lamps, Jardiniers, &c. with various Designs for Rooms, Geometrical and in Perspective, shewing the Decorations, Adjustment of the Furniture, and also some general Observations, and a Description of each Plate. By GEORGE SMITH, Upholder Extraordinary to his Royal Highness the Prince of Wales. Elegantly engraved on 158 Plates, with Descriptions. Royal Quarto, Price 4l. 14s. 6d. in Boards, and elegantly coloured 7l. 17s. 6d.

The Parts may be had Separate, each containing 50 Plates, price 1l. 11s. 6d. each, or elegantly coloured 2l. 12s. 6d.

Designs for *Household Furniture*, exhibiting a Variety of Elegant and Useful Patterns, in the Cabinet, Chair, and Upholstery Branches. By the late *T. Sheraton*. Engraved on 84 Folio Plates, Price 3l. 13s. 6d. in Boards.

Mechanical Exercises; or, the Elements and Practice of Carpentry, Joinery, Bricklaying, Masonry, Slating, Plastering, Painting, Smithing, and Turning. Containing a full Description of the Tools belonging to each Branch of Business, and copious Directions for their Use: with an Explanation of the Terms used in each Art; and an Introduction to Practical Geometry. Illustrated by 39 Plates. By Peter *Nicholson*. Octavo, 18s. Boards, 21s. Bound.

An Essay on the Shafts of Mills; containing their Description and Use, with the Kinds of Stress to which they are subject, and an Inquiry into their Stiffness, Strength, Durability, and Proportion. With a Variety of useful Tables. Also an introductory Account of the Progress and Improvement of MILL-WORK. By *Robertson Buchanan*. Illustrated with Three Plates, Price 7s. Boards.

Essays on the Construction and Durability of the Longitudinal Connexions of Shafts denominated Couplings.—On Methods of Disengaging and Re-engaging Machinery, while in Motion.— On Mechanism for Equalizing the Motion of Mills, denominated Lift-Tenters, Engine Governors, and Water-Wheel Governors.— On the Velocity of Water-Wheels.—On Changing the Velocity of Machinery while in Motion.—On the Framing of Mill-Work. By *Robertson Buchanan*. Illustrated with 15 Plates, Price 12s. in Boards.

Curr's Coal Viewer and Engine Builder's Practical Companion. Quarto, 2l. 12s. 6d.

Smeaton's Experiments on Under-shot and Over-shot Water Wheels, &c. Octavo, with five Plates, 10s. 6d. Boards.

Experimental Enquiries concerning the Principle of the lateral Communication of Motion in Fluids; applied to the Explanation of various Hydraulic Phenomena. By *J. P. Venturi*. Translated from the French by *W. Nicholson*, with Plates, 4s.

A Treatise on the *Teeth of Wheels, Pinions*, &c. demonstrating the best Form which can be given them for the various Purposes of Machinery; such as Mill-work, Clock-work, &c. and the Art of finding their Numbers, translated from the French of *M. Camus*, with Additions, illustrated by 15 Plates, Octavo, 10s. 6d.

Observations on the *Design for the Theatre Royal, Drury Lane*, as executed in the Year 1812; accompanied by Plans, Elevations, and Sections of the same, engraved on Eighteen Plates. By *Benjamin Wyatt*, F. S. A. Architect. Royal Quarto, 2l. 12s. 6d. Boards.

JUST PUBLISHED.

THE ELGIN MARBLES of the Temple of Minerva at Athens, engraved on Sixty-One Plates, selected from Stuart and Revett's Antiquities of Athens; to which are added, the Report from the Select Committee of the House of Commons respecting the Earl of Elgin's Collection of Sculptured Marbles, and an Historical Account of the Temple. Imperial Quarto, Price 5l. 5s. Boards.

Fragments on the *Theory and Practice of Landscape Gardening*, including some Remarks on Grecian and Gothic Architecture, collected from various Manuscripts in the possession of the different Noblemen and Gentlemen for whose Use they were originally written; the Whole tending to establish fixed principles in the respective Arts. By H. *Repton*, Esq., assisted by his Son, *J. Adey Repton*, F.A.S. In Imperial Quarto, illustrated with Fifty-Two Plates, many of them elegantly coloured, uniformly with his former Works, Price 6l. 6s. Boards.

Plans, Elevations, and Sections of Buildings, Public and Private, including Plans and Details of the *New Custom House*, London, with Descriptions. By *David Laing*, Architect. Imperial Folio, Price 4l. 4s. in Boards.

FINIS.

Lightning Source UK Ltd.
Milton Keynes UK
UKHW020638270421
382707UK00004B/149